Reflections of
Keiko Fukuda

Reflections of
Keiko Fukuda

*True Stories from the
Renowned Judo Grand Master*

KUMIKO HIRANO

REFLECTIONS OF KEIKO FUKUDA
TRUE STORIES FROM THE RENOWNED
JUDO GRAND MASTER

iUniverse books may be ordered through booksellers or by contacting:

iUniverse
1663 Liberty Drive
Bloomington, IN 47403
www.iuniverse.com
1-800-Authors (1-800-288-4677)

ISBN: 978-1-5320-3574-6 (sc)
ISBN: 978-1-5320-3573-9 (hc)
ISBN: 978-1-5320-3570-8 (e)

Library of Congress Control Number: 2017918780

Print information available on the last page.

iUniverse rev. date: 01/10/2018

CONTENTS

PREFACE

THE BOOK *BE STRONG, BE Gentle, Be Beautiful* (*Tsuyoku Yasashiku Utsukushiku*) was published in Japan. This is the translation of that book. It is the story of Keiko Fukuda Shihan, who began her passage to become a judo master at the age of twenty-two in 1935. As the only woman in the world to achieve the level of tenth *dan*, she blazed the way for women in judo to be taken seriously across all martial arts arenas, including the Olympics. I hope this book will help readers understand Master Fukuda's great spirit and her dedication to judo and all judo enthusiasts.

It was February 2012 when I had a long interview with Master Keiko Fukuda. The interview lasted about four hours per day and was conducted over the course of a week at her home in San Francisco. I was part of a news crew filming a documentary on her life as the last living student of Grand Master Jigoro Kano, founder of the Kodokan Judo Institute near Tokyo. She was nearly one hundred years old, with a clear and vivid memory, and her passion and devotion to judo had not changed at all since her youth.

In the following pages, I will present a narration in Keiko's voice, as if she is speaking to us directly. The reader will encounter a number of stories from Keiko's point of view. These are the stories that chart the course of a remarkable journey to enlightenment through the study of judo.

There is a proverb—"bear most, hang lowest in Japan." No matter how gifted you are, you can't improve your techniques or personality without making strenuous efforts. Master Fukuda's motto, "be strong, be gentle, be beautiful," is the result of her untiring training.

There is a glossary at the back of the book for reference to specific terms named in this book.

Kumiko Hirano, December 2015

ONE

San Francisco

(Translator note: She was very honored that an entire news crew would travel so far just to meet and talk to her.)

I OPENED THE SOKO JOSHI Judo Club on Castro Street in San Francisco back in 1973 …

"Soko" is written with the Japanese letters of a mulberry tree and a harbor, and translated means San Francisco. My dojo is the whole first floor of the building, and I think it is about thirty-four tatami mats wide. A locker room is beside the dojo. The first location was here at my residence in the basement in 1967.

The picture displayed on the front wall is judo master Mr. Jigoro Kano (1860–1938). Although young people may not know, he was the founder of the Kodokan Judo Institute, an excellent teacher, and a great person who spread judo all over the world. Even though I started my formal judo studies just three years before his death,

I knew of him from family history of my grandfather as his most promising student.

The portrait displayed next to him is my grandfather Hachinosuke Fukuda (1828–1879). I think this is a copy of the original that somebody found because my family didn't have any of his photographs in my home.

Because my grandfather was a jujitsu master in the Tenjinshinyo School, he taught soldiers of the shogunate in the Edo era. Kano sensei, who was an Empire Tokyo University student, became a student of my grandfather's dojo in the Meiji era.

Kano sensei learned traditional techniques of jujitsu from three jujitsu teachers and then created judo by combining three elements: physical education, competition, and cultivation of the mind to strengthen the body. While I didn't know my grandfather because he died way before I was born, Kano sensei was my first judo teacher and my guide in life.

Soon after I started my life in San Francisco, I taught judo in the basement of Shelley's house (Dr. Shelley Fernandez) in 1967. She became my life partner. It was about ten tatami mats wide. In the beginning, about ten students came to me from the school where Shelley worked. Shortly after that, a lot of students came, and her house became too small to practice judo. We finally rented a practice space at the Sokoji Zen Temple in Japantown. Then a lot of second- and third-generation Japanese girls came to practice judo.

Because we practiced at a temple, the Buddhist mortuary tablets fell down on the floor if we practiced a throwing technique too many times. We practiced very carefully. After two years, we moved to 1622 Castro Street.

Because I was born in 1913 (Taisho 2nd), I became ninety-nine years old on April 12, 2012. I am already a hundred years old, counting in the traditional Japanese way. If I had lived in Japan all through my life, I wouldn't have had a dojo like this and wouldn't be able to do judo at my age. Because I heard it has been cold and sometimes snowing in Tokyo lately, I, first and foremost, wouldn't be alive [gently laughing]. I am thankful that it is mild and comfortable to live in San Francisco.

It has been more than forty-five years since I came here, San Francisco, in 1966 (Showa 41st). Although I came here without knowing what kind of people lived in San Francisco, unexpectedly it has been comfortable for me to live here. Even so, I never dreamed that I might live outside of Japan for so many years. At the beginning, I never thought this was it for my life, but I always thought about how I could follow Kano sensei's heart once I became a student.

After all, everything was difficult for women at that time because they had to choose either judo or marriage, not both. Traditional Japan allowed women to work, but if they chose marriage, they were expected to quit their jobs to be subservient, obedient, and passive but hard workers for the good of the family. Devotion was key. Judo was like a job. On no account could you ever have both. But I never thought about marriage. I thought about nothing but judo. I am as if I am married to judo.

I will gradually talk about how my life was determined. It is as though I followed my destiny.

The things on the wall are letters of thanks given from all over America and clubs in the world, a testimonial by two mayors, and promotion certificates. I have received so many honors over the years, and I think I received too many. I even received a decoration from the Japanese government as a sacred treasure of Japan. This great honor is far more than I deserve.

Since the traditional Kodokan was conservative, women couldn't get more than fifth dan. It was naturally thought there was no need to give women more than that. It was banned for women to play a match too. Because of that, since I was promoted to fifth dan in 1953 (Showa 28th), my rank remained for a long time. My partner, Shelley, convinced the Kodokan to raise me and all women to sixth dan.

When I came to America, men and women were equal here. The judo associations in America gave me the tenth dan I think because they appreciated that I made a contribution to the development of judo in America and taught judo for women in different countries. But a Yawara heart isn't influenced by a dan title. So I never argued with Kodokan's way of thinking or the policy. The most important thing is a cultivated heart, a practice as a good human being.

I heard that I am the only female who held tenth dan. I was

very happy that a lot of people gathered and celebrated for me in October 2011. Even before I was given ninth dan from Kodokan in 2006 (Heisei 18th), the USA and USJF Associations in America, my students, and a lot of people supported me and tried to impress on them that I deserved it. I am fortunate.

The training schedule is three times a week, from 6:00 p.m. to 8:00 p.m. on Tuesday and Thursday and from 10:00 a.m. to 12:00 p.m. on Saturday. Although it may be way longer training than other dojos do, when I practiced under training by Grand Master Kano, it was three hours a day from Monday through Saturday, from 3:00 p.m. to 6:00 p.m. on Monday through Friday and from 2:00 p.m. to 5:00 p.m. on Saturday. His students started cleaning up his dojo thirty minutes before training. He strictly taught us manners and the way of speaking.

The word *dojo*, widely used in judo, comes from Buddhism, and it means "a place to train." So when I teach judo for foreign students, I make sure to begin my teaching with talking about manners.

Whenever we come in and leave the dojo, we respectfully bow to the mat. We bow to the front when we come back from and go to a locker room too. We have to be respectful to our teachers and seniors, and students also bow to each other. These manners are very important.

I start training with bows, saying, "Bow to our teacher" and "Bow to the front (meaning to Shihan Kano and my grandfather)," and we end it with another bow, saying, "Thank you very much" after a short meditation sitting upright in Seiza style. The orders are all in Japanese. I teach technical terms of judo, like the category of Waza in Japanese, of course.

I appreciate that students from any country follow this way once

I teach it. It is true that some dojos don't care about manners. But my dojo is different. No cross-legged sitting at all.

In America, many people sit cross-legged because they've never been taught the correct position. Students who came from different dojos sit cross-legged while they are chatting after training. If they have black belts, I can't believe it, can I? They can't sit upright in Seiza style just because they didn't learn to sit in that way. So I teach students like them how they can sit in Seiza style step by step. Women seem beautiful when they are well behaved in the old-fashioned manner. When I teach correctly, most students can do it. No problem at all.

We do warm-up exercises very carefully. I assign my students to repeatedly practice basic movements of judo until they can do them through and through. If they don't practice with all the energy, they can't master the positions, can they? Every kind of training is like that, isn't it? And then we will practice ju-no-kata and randori. These two are necessary to get the judo skills. Ju-no-kata is the mechanics before the throw. Randori is two students practicing both defense and offense using Waza, judo techniques.

Since my dojo is for women, I teach self-defense techniques too. Quite a few people have become students of my dojo because they wanted to learn self-defense techniques. I am wondering if it is of specific interest in America.

I also assign students to repeatedly practice a throwing technique and a defensive fall. If they master the technique of the defensive fall, they won't be injured or be afraid. Shelley told me that one of my students was hit by a car and flew fifteen feet onto the road. Thanks to mastering those techniques, she ended up with only minor injuries.

On training days, Shelley or my students take me to the dojo and pick me up. Because all of them have good character, they take care of me very gently. I am fortunate. Some people may think I don't have to be sorry but deserve their support as a return favor because I've taken care of a lot of my students, but I don't think so. I can't help being sorry because I don't have many things I can do for them anymore.

Several years ago, I was able to show model examples of Waza on a mat and did warm-up exercises with my students. Recently I have only observed their practice and given advice while sitting in a chair because my leg muscles have weakened. Even though my body has weakened, I like teaching. Moreover, a judo uniform naturally guides me to pay attention to judo. When I am in the uniform, I feel as if my spirit is inspired, and my backbone is stretched out.

Recently, most of my students in this dojo have been single. There are twenty or more students. Some of them have earned third dan, fourth dan, and fifth dan.

Students come to practice judo not only from America but also from different countries, like India, Russia, Mexico, China, and England. Some practiced karate or yoga before judo, and some already practiced judo in the army of their own country.

In Japan, housewives don't commonly practice judo, but here people continue judo after their marriage. However, once they have children, many of them leave the dojo because they can't come to practice in the evening.

Lately, I've spoken in Japanese in spite of myself when I teach students. They don't understand my Japanese and say, "Sensei, English, please," but Japanese naturally comes out from my mouth.

A while ago, I was hospitalized for a few days. When I came back from the hospital, the students gave me a TV set so that I could watch Japanese TV programs. They thought I wouldn't be bored but would be able to have quiet rest for my health. Since then, I have watched Japanese TV programs every day and lost English words. I've become such a Japanese language teacher who holds tenth dan. It has now made a great sensation in my dojo.

— Makeup Gives Me Willpower —

Judo has been the center of my life for a long time. Because I think only about judo, I don't think my daily life interests you at all. But if you don't mind, may I talk about my daily life?

This district is called Noe Valley. Although it takes about thirty minutes by car from downtown San Francisco, it is calm and comfortable for me to live. There are mainly houses, so the atmosphere is peaceful.

I've lived in this house for more than forty years. It's not bad to see out from the balcony because I can see different neighborhoods around the whole Bay Area, and small birds often visit here. I used to be able to walk the hill unconcernedly, but I can't often go out with my weaker legs now. I used to go grocery shopping in Japantown to buy Japanese ingredients once a month, but I can't do that either, unless Shelley is with me.

When I have time, I often sit down on this sofa in this room facing the balcony and watch TV and read judo magazines. I sometimes take a nap on this sofa.

The portrait of me above the sofa was painted by a famous artist (Dr. Andor Paposi-Jobb). It, *2005—WMJA Championship, Mississauga, Ontario, Canada*, was completed and sent to me before I knew of it. I heard that he got inspiration when he watched my judo somewhere, and then he decided to paint me. I think it's a good picture done well, isn't it?

Portrait of Keiko by Dr. Paposi

I usually wake up at 9:00 a.m. After washing my face, I put on makeup, dress myself, and comb my hair. It takes about ten minutes. Makeup gives me the feeling of agelessness and energetic. I go to a beauty salon to have my hair dyed once a month. It is refreshing too.

I have used Shiseido cosmetics for a long time. I use a toner and a lotion after washing my face. I've been using the same cosmetics for about sixty years. I think it's good for my skin. When I go to the Shiseido shop, they automatically bring what I want. It's convenient, isn't it?

When I went to Los Angeles, I forget exactly when though, somebody I didn't know suddenly asked me, "What on earth do you do to take care of your skin?" My skin was so soft and smooth that she was curious about what cosmetics I used. I said, "I don't do anything special." Although I say makeup, my makeup has been just powdering a little bit since I was young. It is right for my age now. But makeup still gives me a good feeling.

Then I come down to the kitchen from the upstairs and eat breakfast around ten. I have toast, fruit, and a cup of coffee. I had a banana this morning. I sometimes have a hardboiled egg and sometimes bacon and eggs.

I used to cook rice and miso soup by myself. Since it is easy to get regular Japanese ingredients in Japantown, I used to cook *chawan-mushi*, *niku-jaga*, *gomaae*, rolling sushi, and so on when I had time. I cooked a lot of those meals and gave them to others. They liked my cooking very much because it's home cooking that they wouldn't have at Japanese restaurants. I do everything quickly. Because I like cooking, I cooked everything quickly too.

Even now, I sometimes want to eat rice with *natto* and miso soup as a breakfast, but I haven't cooked rice anymore since I physically can't move like I could before. Because I don't cook rice, I can't eat it. I don't eat even my favorite tofu lately. I eat the same breakfast as Shelley eats. We usually eat Western food. First of all, Americans cannot make miso soup, right? I usually eat breakfast that Shelley makes for me, so I've become as if I were American if somebody looks at what I eat.

After breakfast, I sometimes turn on a Japanese TV channel, NHK, to do exercises with its program and listen to old pop songs. My schedule depends on my health condition on the day, but I never miss judo. I'm not so relaxed because many different people have been coming to see me since I got tenth dan, the highest degree of judo. My niece told me that it was reported in Japan too. That's why.

I usually eat Japanese food for lunch. Sometimes I get a Japanese-style grilled fish bento box, and sometimes I get a roast chicken or a spaghetti bento box. It's convenient to get them because there are a lot of restaurants where I can buy a to-go box around here. Shelley buys a lot of food and puts it into a freezer in the American fashion. I think American people don't mind if they reheat frozen food in a microwave and eat it every day.

After lunch, I sometimes take a nap, read a judo magazine, write a letter, and watch NHK programs; for example, *Nodo Jiman*, an amateur singing contest program and a pop song program. I am glad if I have some *osen*, rice crackers, for a snack. I've liked osen very much since I was a child. I like any kind of osen if it is the real thing.

I sometimes watch sumo wrestling on TV, but I am disappointed that foreign sumo wrestlers are active and Japanese sumo wrestlers are weak. Only a person who has a strong will can win. It is exactly the same as judo.

While I am watching a Japanese TV program, sometimes Shelley is watching an English or a Spanish TV program in another room. It may seem comical sharing life, doesn't it?

Because I teach judo lessons on Tuesday evening and Thursday evening as well as Saturday morning, even if I take a nap, I surely wake up by 5:00 p.m. Shelley and my students who have black belts come and help me to change my clothes at 5:00 p.m. I don't like to wear a wrinkled judo uniform. Some American people don't fold clothes after taking them off.

The red belt that I use now was given by the USJF Judo Federation for celebrating my long life on my ninetieth birthday. I usually wear two bracelets. The bead bracelet was sent all the way from Brazil by Brazilian judo sensei Roberto Resende. I don't know the person very well. This silver ring was given by my friend who cooks Christmas dinner for me every year.

My job is to wear a judo uniform and go to the dojo three times a week. I learned not only judo from Kano sensei but also the way of living as a human being. Whether I do judo or not, his teaching is always in my heart. And no matter how much I need physical help, I am a part of society. I hope to use my ability effectively for society.

When I have a lesson that I teach, I eat dinner after teaching. It's about nine o'clock. When I don't have a lesson, I have dinner about seven. I usually eat Western food; for example, meat loaf or roast chicken. I sometimes eat out. I like Japanese food, of course, because I am Japanese. There is my favorite sushi restaurant, Hamano Sushi, near here, and I have gone there since they opened. I like *chirashi* sushi and *maguro* sushi. The taste depends on what sushi items they purchased for the day. The owner is very kind to me.

Everyone is surprised that I have a good appetite. I was trained to respect and eat all food. I try to eat it all.

I go to bed about eleven. Yes, my everyday life is like this now.

----------------------------------- **Life Partner That God Decided** —

I came to San Francisco in 1966 (Showa 41st), met Shelley, and started living with her.

This is my nature to think, *It's all right*, if someone asks me, "Let's live together." However, I have never been asked like that by a man.

Because I'm not so social and basically I have thought about judo all the time since I came here, I didn't have much time for anything else. I didn't have anyone around me who gave me advice about my marriage, nor someone special for me. Now I am happy that I didn't have such a person.

When I met Shelley, she was already a beginner judo student at the Koyukan Dojo in San Francisco. She came to see me in person because she had heard that a female judo teacher came from the Kodokan in Japan. Hattori sensei, a Japanese teacher, introduced me to her. Because I could speak broken English, we became friends as I taught her judo.

In the year I met her, she said she'd just lost her mother. She said my personality was very similar to her mother. She might feel close to me because of that.

My personality is different from hers, so we sometimes go back and forth in Japanese and English if something is uncomfortable. People have likes and dislikes; so do we. Because we both are openhearted, it works. She is full of fun and mischief too. She registered the number of her license plate "JUDOKF9" for judo rank.

She rarely cooks. I assume the reason we started living together was I cooked for her. On the other hand, she studies very hard. She was a schoolteacher with an important post in California. She devoted herself to women's rights activity. She has been interested in politics. Anyway, she is a brilliant person who is very different from me. Whenever she comes near my ear, she says, "I'll talk to you in Japanese, and you try to talk to me in English." I just say, "Okay, sure" [gently laughing]. I appreciate my good fortune in meeting her because she made it easier for me to adapt to life in America naturally.

I think it was fate meeting her because I have lived with her for this long time.

She is originally from New York, so I think her family members live there. Her daughter, who lives on the other side of the Golden Gate Bridge, sometimes comes to see us and helps with chores. She is very helpful because she is a good cook, unlike her mother.

It's because of Shelley's total support for me that I could start teaching judo in America. Thanks to her, I could get citizenship too.

I appreciate her from my heart because she has fully supported me. God must have decided for us to live together, didn't he? We might be born under the same star.

We are now like sisters. I wonder how many years we are different … I believe she is seventeen or eighteen years younger than me. She teasingly says *onesama* (my dear older sister). Since I received tenth dan, she's said she must call me a grand master.

TWO

❖

Youth

MY GRANDFATHER HACHINOSUKE FUKUDA WAS a jujitsu master.
He was born and raised as a second son in a farming family in
Musashikoku Chichibugun (which is now Saitama prefecture) in
the Ansei year of the Edo era (1854–1860). His original name was
Chiyokichi Mochida. He'd been tall, about six feet (about 160 cm)
and strong since he was a child. I heard nobody could beat him at
sumo wrestling. While he trained in jujitsu under a jujitsu teacher
in a rural district, he wanted to go to Edo (Tokyo), train in jujitsu,
and have wider knowledge and experiences. My grandmother said
he moved to Edo without his parents' knowledge.

There were dojos of various schools in Edo, and he trained at a
Tenjinshinyo School dojo in Kandaotamagaike in Edo.

While he developed his skills, he was recommended to be a
teacher at Edo shogunate martial art training school. However, he
was not a samurai warrior but a son of a farming family, so it wasn't
possible for him to get the job. So, I think, he was adopted by

Fukuda, who was his teacher's wife's relative, changed his name to Hachinosuke Fukuda, and got hired as a jujitsu teacher at the martial arts training school. I heard the training school was in what is now Kanda Ogawacho. While he taught jujitsu for shogunate soldiers, he had his own dojo in Motodaikucho, Nihonbashi Ward. After becoming a master, he named himself "Ryugizai, Hachinosuke Fukuda, Masayoshi Minamoto."

When the world totally changed after the Meiji era started, samurai warriors went out of business, the military arts became old-fashioned, and then many jujitsu experts found themselves in financial difficulties. Because they could not feed their families, I heard that they gave up their dojos and became osteopaths. However, my grandfather kept his dojo and also worked as an osteopath in order to live.

My grandmother said that Jigoro Kano sensei, who was a student at the Tokyo Imperial University, visited my grandfather's dojo with a referral in about Meiji 10th (1877). He wanted to be stronger by learning judo because he was short and weak. He scouted for a dojo that taught traditional Japanese martial arts techniques. So when he finally found my grandfather's dojo, his dream had come true.

After he became my grandfather's student, he trained very hard every single day. His skills developed very quickly. When the former American president Ulysses S. Grant visited as the US ambassador to Japan at the end of his world tour in Meiji 12th (1879), Eiichi Shibusawa, a businessman, invited President Grant to his house in Asuka Mountain (Kitaoji in Tokyo) and demonstrated traditional Japanese jujitsu for him. My grandfather and other judo experts performed there. Kano sensei was also one of them and showed randori with other students who had more experience.

My grandparents had eight children, but five of them died when they were children. My father, Ryukichi, is a second son. My father wasn't related to jujitsu but a businessman stocking and selling rice. My mother is Tatsu. Her parents owned a famous chinaware store by Koshu Road. I heard that they gave a lot of chinaware bearing the signature of the store to nearby farming families.

My grandfather had a stroke and died not longer than ten days after he demonstrated jujitsu for President Grant. He was fifty-two years old. Because all his children were small—my father was nine years old—my grandmother went through many hardships to raise her children. Although his dojo was closed because of his sudden death, the Hereditary Book on Tenjinshinyo School was handed over to Kano sensei. I think my grandmother trusted him because he trained both kata, or form, and randori, and also he was the best student in the dojo even though some other students had trained longer than he had.

Kano sensei trained under Masatomo Iso, a master of Tenjinshinyo School, and Tsunetoshi Iikubo, a master of Kito School, after my grandfather's death. Then he created "judo," which is more logical and more mentally meaningful than jujitsu. It was in Meiji 15th (1882), three years after my grandfather's death, that he finally started Kodokan at a temple in Shimoya (what is now Ueno Daitouku in Tokyo). I was happy to know his original place to teach judo was a temple because I also rented a temple to teach judo before I started my dojo on Castro Street.

My grandmother, who was from a samurai warrior family, was working at Edo Castle before her marriage. I don't know the details about it, but her occupation was like a maid in the women's quarters in the castle. Because of that, she was proud and strict about speaking and manners. I had to sit in Seiza style the whole time and was scolded if I showed my foot under my hip. I was nervous in front of her because my mother would be scolded by my grandmother if I did something improperly. She called Kano sensei just "Kano" without the title. She also sometimes visited his dojo. Because of the way she treated him, I didn't know that he was such a great judo master.

She died when she was eighty-two years old, and I was twelve years old.

— **Early Years** —

The house where I was born was near Nihonbashi in Tokyo. I had five siblings: two elder sisters, an elder brother, and a younger sister. However, the second sister died when she was fifteen or sixteen years old. My brother was physically weak and often got sick, so he and his old caretaker went to a place where the air was clean; for example, Atami along the coast in Shizuoka. As a result, he couldn't learn jujitsu and judo.

I was left with a farming family and raised by them until I turned five or six years old. I lived with the family in Someya, which is far from Nihonbashi. When I talk about this, Shelley says that Japanese at that time had a different approach to raising their children. I understand that my parents left me with the family because they hoped for me to be healthy, unlike my brother. At that time, there were ways for farm families to make money by raising other families' children.

My mother visited and brought clothes for me in spring and autumn. I also sometimes visited my house, but I wasn't attached to her because I felt she didn't seem like my real mother. I hardly remember what my life in the farming family was like now. I might drink goat milk and play free from all cares in the country. I returned to my house one year before I entered an elementary school.

I was an honor student from second grade through sixth grade. Because I was already a hard worker, I went to school every day and studied very hard. When I graduated from the school, I received graduation certificates on behalf of all the students, and I received commendations too. I was also skillful with my fingers and was good at handcrafts.

I survived the Great Kanto earthquake of 1923 when I was in the fifth grade, ten years old. Because a lot of students older than me left the school due to the earthquake, I came to represent the other students who stayed. Even I was surprised at how much I had progressed.

What I was most surprised by in the aftermath of the quake was that houses were destroyed as if they were built out of sand. Because traditional houses were enclosed with mud walls, sand fell from all directions like rain whenever the ground shook. I was very, very frightened.

It was about noon, and my father was out. Since there were only women in my house, managers and young helpers came from my mother's original home to help us. A young helper carried my grandmother, who couldn't walk well, on his back, and managers took important documents out for us. A couple who lived in one of the houses for rent on our premises took my sister and me and rushed to an emergency evacuation area in Miyashiro Park in front of the Imperial Palace.

Orange-colored fire followed us while we were running away. I heard in the emergency evacuation area that a stretch of Nihonbashi area was quickly burned to the ground. Some people saw many people who had died, one upon another. All the houses for rent that my family owned were burned to the ground too, and nothing remained. Because everybody was burned out in the fire, and many families left the place they had gotten to know, only six students could return to my class at the school. Because my family lost our house, we lived in my mother's original house for a while. I'm wondering how we lived after that … I think we moved to a rural area. We rented a house until we found a house where all my family could settle down. My brother, who was physically weak, stayed in the countryside with his caretakers for a while.

After life in the rental house, we moved to Noborito in Kanagawa prefecture and rented about ten thousand square feet of land. Since I lived near Ginza, a central area in Tokyo, I thought I had moved to a different environment from the place where I had lived.

A neighbor who was from Shinshu, in the northeastern area of Japan, recommended that my brother keep goats. I think my brother thought that taking the goats to the Tama riverbank would be good exercise for him and that drinking goat milk would make him healthier. He started running a goat ranch by renting goats.

He closed the ranch because the Sino-Japanese War raged. After the war, he started running an inn using a bachelor's apartment he had built on the same land. Even now, my nephew Akimitsu and his wife keep the inn in Noborito peninsula in Ishikawa. It is called Hotel Fukudaya.

Since my grandfather and father left the family a lot of rental houses, we all had a comfortable life and went to school instead of work. As was the custom, we saw little of real life. I started learning to play shamisen, a three-stringed Japanese banjo, when I was six. I lived with my aunt who had come back to her parents' house because her married life hadn't gone well. Although she liked shamisen, she never learned it, so instead she made me learn it with a shamisen master in Nihonbashi. My grandmother and my mother said that I needed skills. Generally speaking, all girls would get married at marriageable ages, so they might have thought having skills would rather help my marriage.

When I went to see the shamisen master with my aunt, I was too small to carry a shamisen on my knees. It was so hard to finger the strings too. Without her supporting my fingers, I couldn't make any sound. I continued practicing it until I went to a girls' school. I practiced shamisen so much every day at home that the wife of a nearby shop owner who sold wooden clogs memorized "Tokiwazu," a piece of music that I practiced.

I brought my shamisen to America and played it very often. It was very good solace when I missed Japan. However, lately I hardly play it. I have left it by the fireplace because I can't make the right tone without tuning the strings section.

In addition to the shamisen, I also practiced calligraphy. The same aunt went on about it that women have to write letters for their husbands and have to have good handwriting. She introduced me to a calligraphy teacher who graduated from the same school as she did. Thus, I started learning calligraphy too.

In my marriageable age, I learned Japanese flower arrangement and the tea ceremony. In addition, I learned general sewing and cooking. I trained for married life as other ordinary girls did. My mother worried about my marriage, but I didn't think about marriage in my marriageable age. My mother supported me financially to learn those lessons; however, she didn't allow me to buy luxuries.

I reached the turning point of my life before my twenty-first birthday.

When the fiftieth anniversary of the Kodokan that Kano sensei started was held at the new Kodokan in Koishikawa (what is now Bunkyoku) on March 3, Showa 9th (1934), my mother, my brother, and my aunt were invited. Nobody in my family did judo, and my grandfather had died when my father was nine years old, so our family hadn't had any acquaintance with him or with the Kodokan for a long time. Then my mother and my brother received the courteous invitations, and they were so surprised.

At the anniversary, Kano sensei dedicated three sakaki trees as spirits of his three masters, Hachinosuke Fukuda (my grandfather), Masatomo Iso, and Tsunetosi Iikubo from Kito School. Especially when he talked to my grandfather's sakaki tree, he fondly talked to my grandfather's spirit and showed his gratitude.

My brother talked to me about what he saw. He said that Kano sensei talked to my grandfather as if he were alive. He said, "A tear rolled down, and my heart was full of deep emotion."

It might have been the day after the ceremony that Kano sensei visited and brought a fiftieth anniversary memento to our house in Noborito all the way from Tokyo. When he arrived at our house, I glanced in a pocket of his jacket hanging in the entrance hall, and there were chocolates and candies.

When I served tea for him, I met him. Although I had heard he was a grand master, I didn't feel he was scary because my grandmother used to call him "Kano, Kano" without the title, and he wasn't so big but skinny. When I greeted him, he said, "You look like Ryu san (Ryukichi, my father)." While I was wondering if I looked like my father so much, he said with a smile, "Why don't you come to the Kodokan because we have the women's department?"

Several months later, because he had encouraged me to do judo and become healthier, my mother took me to the Kodokan women's department.

When I observed judo for the first time, I was surprised to see such showy exercises, with the bodies moving aggressively. As I said before, my grandmother strictly trained me in manners, so I've never sat casually. However, the girls were standing with their legs spread and throwing other girls. I was stunned that judo required such wild movements.

After I came back home, I was wondering many things, such as if I could do such exercises, and that the practices might be very hard. My mother and my brother never said I should learn judo, but I thought that my family was related to the Kodokan and that it might be good for my health. Then my uncle was against the idea because he thought women should not do judo. However, I have decided everything by myself since I was a small child. When I decide, my decision is strong. So nobody can say anything to me. At that time, too, I finally decided by myself to become a student of the Kodokan. It was in Showa 10th (1935).

Because my father passed away at his early age, my mother was worried about me, as I was now of marriageable age. When I became a student there, she asked Kano sensei to find a prospective marriage partner for me. She probably trusted him to find and introduce a suitable man for me because he was a principal of a high school in Tokyo and had a wide circle of acquaintances. I assume that she permitted me to become a student of the Kodokan with her own purpose of getting me married.

I took trains on the Odakyu line and Sho line (the Department of Railway, Japan National Railway, the forerunner of JR) to go to the Kodokan from my house in Noborito. I first went to Shinjuku by the Odakyu line, changed to the Sho line, got off at Suidobashi station, and walked for a while.

The head manager of the women's department was Noriko Watanuki, Kano sensei's oldest daughter. The training chief was Yoshimaro Handa sensei, who had seventh dan. The director was Takashi Usawa, who held fourth dan, and the training assistant was Masako Noritomi, who taught beginners.

I would team up with Noritomi sensei, my senpai (a person who has more experience), to demonstrate ju-no-kata. She was from Fukuoka. When she was training judo hard at a rural dojo, Kiichiro Sato, an instructor in the Kodokan found her, and she became a student after that. She was an old live-in student in Kano sensei's house and rendered service to judo training for women. She passed away long ago though …

The women's training room was close to Kano sensei's room, and he sometimes dropped in the training room and made some requests to instructors. I heard that he had his first female student in the Meiji era, and he found his teaching style by trial and error. In the following Taisho era, some girls' schools started teaching judo here and there. The Kodokan women's department officially started in the late Taisho era, and there were about ten students when I became a student.

The schedule was three-hour training every day from Monday through Friday. Students cleaned the dojo thirty minutes before the training, and he strictly trained the manner and the way of speaking as well. He even more strictly trained us in manners because we had to consider femininity important, unlike the men's dojo. While we trained, a war widow was in a chair at the corner of our dojo and pointed out when we were acting improperly. Nobody was allowed to misbehave—for example, going into a store, chatting with friends, or eating sweets on the way back from the dojo—and nobody broke the rules.

I heard that the reason he started the women's department in Taisho 15th (1926) was he thought it was good for women to learn the art of self-defense and to have physical and mental strength when they became mothers. In addition, he thought that women who were physically less strong than men would be the ideal people for the original concept of gentle judo. Practice for women never pushed them too hard. I never trained in groundwork techniques requiring physical strength, but I learned mainly about techniques that make use of the women's flexibility. Those techniques are so reasonable that each one is beautiful and gentle.

I continuously practiced ju-no-kata and randori. It's important to practice until it becomes automatic, so we voluntarily practiced those on the mat that we spread on the rooftop of the Kodokan.

These days, both men and women train with equal effort and practice the same judo. It is necessary for them to win a match. Women's judo changed so much.

Once I became a student, instructors who had higher dan said, "She is Hachinosuke Fukuda's granddaughter," and, "Master Kano's master's granddaughter came to be a student," and they were very good to me. Male teachers were kind to me in a respectful way. I felt so glad for such thoughtfulness.

However, the atmosphere in the women's department was slightly different. A student who started judo when she was ten years old acted "big" probably because she was the first judo instructor of the women's department. I felt she was protecting her position as the number-one assistant. She might have had to behave in an authoritative manner as a female judo expert.

When I got the second dan in Showa 15th (1940), she clearly said, "You are not eligible for the second dan. You got the second dan even though you can't do enough judo." Once she scolded me, saying, "Why can't you do this technique?" even though I hadn't learned the technique. When newspaper journalists came to cover us, they were sure to ask each of us, "Why did you start judo?" Then other students made sarcastic remarks, saying, "Because you have good lineage, they are just excited about it." The criticism was relatively severe, but there was nothing for me to do because I was Hachinosuke Fukuda's granddaughter. I realized from the experience that I had to accept that I was born in such a family. Even then, I wasn't very much worried about it and just practiced very hard, and then I got the third dan in Showa 17th (1942). Three students had higher positions at the Kodokan women's department; Noritomi sensei was the first, I was the second, and Haruko Niboshi was the third.

Before the war, women from ordinary families couldn't become students of the women's department; only women from upper-class families could. Their way of speaking was also snobby. Although my grandmother strictly trained me in manners, I still spoke in the common Tokyo dialect. So I was at a loss at the beginning. I gradually got used to it when women said, "I'd like to apologize. Did it hurt you?" when they merely bumped against the other person's foot during practice. Because Kano sensei's granddaughter was also a student there, other students might have been even more careful.

Soon after I became a student, I made friends with Ms. Kitaoka, who was a year younger than me and was a daughter of a vice captain of a vessel for the Showa emperor. I also became a friend with Ms. Tanaka, who was from Hawaii. There was an international atmosphere since the Kodokan welcomed students from foreign places, such as Indonesia, England, and Hawaii. Ms. Tanaka went to an English school while she learned Judo.

I have pleasant memories of them since we always practiced and chatted together. We gathered at the Kodokan for national holidays, such as the Meiji Memorial Day (the Meiji emperor's birthday) and the Tencho Memorial Day (the Showa emperor's birthday), and we took one-day trips to Nagatoro (Saitama prefecture) and the Murayama Reservoir (Tama Lake in Daitowa City, Tokyo), and we practiced.

Kano sensei was extremely busy attending many international conferences and energetically playing an active role abroad. Therefore, he rarely taught us judo at the Kodokan. When he did teach us, he didn't wear the judo uniform but a suit. However, he repeatedly taught us his spiritual theory of "using energy for good purposes and sharing mutual prosperity."

He said to us, students of the women's department, that he hoped that women would go abroad and spread judo over the world. His talks immediately encouraged us to start learning English. We really hoped to be loyal to his aim.

Kano sensei suddenly died on May 4 in Showa 13th (1938).

I was so shocked when I heard the news. I had some feeling that I couldn't describe. Because I hoped an excellent person like him would live a long life, I was so sorry for him.

He had been extremely busy visiting all over the world so that the Tokyo Olympic Games in Showa 15th (1940) would come true. As the result of his effort, but just before he died, Tokyo was chosen for the next Olympic Games at the general meeting of the IOC (the International Olympic Committee) in Cairo, Egypt. After the meeting in Cairo, he had flown to Europe, America, and Canada, and then returned from Vancouver by the ship *Hikawamaru*. However, his cold worsened to pneumonia, and he died just as the ship was arriving at Yokohama Harbor. I heard that everybody rushed to the harbor from the Kodokan and carried his body home.

His funeral was held at the Kodokan in Koishikawa. It was

magnificent. He was a person who had held many different jobs, including as a member of the House of Peers and as an educator. He worked hard not only for Japan but also for the world. Many eminent people in Japan, from the prime minister to career officers, attended the funeral.

Judo magazines reported the funeral, and some students of the women's department were in some of the pictures. I keep photographs of the funeral as my treasures. I visited his grave on the first anniversary of his death.

I more firmly resolved to continue judo after the death of the one who had led me to the judo world. I realized once again that I was born in the Fukuda family. It is greatly significant for me that my grandfather was a jujitsu master of Jigoro Kano.

The more I hoped to continue judo in the future, the more I realized I didn't have much education. Because I had failed the entrance examination of a public middle school after I graduated from elementary school, I went to private schools: Kojicho Girls' School (Kojicho girls' middle and high school) and the dressmaking department of Tokyo Domestic Science School (Tokyo Domestic Science University). However, I hoped to study more and understand more about "using energy for good purposes and sharing mutual prosperity," the spirit of judo that Kano sensei always talked about. I finally entered the preparatory course of the department of Japanese literature at Japan Women Advanced School (Showa Women's University) with a recommendation by Kano sensei's daughter, who was the manager of the women's department. Because judo is one of the most important martial arts, I expected I would improve my understanding through learning calligraphy and Japanese history.

I graduated from the preparatory course and transferred to the regular course in Showa 18th (1943). When I had completed my studies and was about to graduate, I was drafted into the war effort. Yet I am happy I could go to the university like others. Thinking about that again, if I had chosen the department of English literature, I wouldn't have had difficulties with the English language, nor had to feel ashamed when I taught judo abroad. Many years later, I did receive my diploma from Showa Women's University.

THREE

Marriage or Judo

SOME PEOPLE MIGHT LOOK WITH curiosity at women learning judo, and others might think it's an option only for upper-class girls. However, I appreciate judo because I became physically strong and healthy by going to the dojo every day. I was promoted to a higher dan after about five years of practice, and I began to receive a salary from the Kodokan.

I began to demonstrate ju-no-kata at championship tournaments and other tournaments in rural areas after I got the first dan in Showa 14th (1939). Ju-no-kata has systematic positions combined with many judo techniques, such as Kuzushi, defensive body movement, and use of power.

Whenever I went to different places with the director of the Kodokan and teachers who held higher dans, I demonstrated ju-no-kata with Masako Noritomi sensei. She usually played as "Tori," the role of the person who does the throwing, and I, who had less experience, played as "Uke," the person to be thrown.

I was already twenty-six or twenty-seven years old. The traditional Japanese viewpoint was that women of such ages had to get married. However, I was deeper in my new experiences and judo techniques and not thinking whether to get married or to continue judo. I overcame my physical weakness, and I seldom caught a cold because of my judo training.

At this time, Ms. Kitaoka, who was my good friend, received an offer of marriage.

As I told you, I was close friend with Ms. Tanaka, who was from Hawaii, and Ms. Kitaoka, whose father was a vice captain of a vessel for the Showa emperor, and I was always with them. When my good friend's marriage is about to happen, even if I am the best friend, I can't say what is none of my business, like you should not marry, or you had better marry. Finally, well-bred and beautiful Ms. Kitaoka quit judo and married.

When I became a student of the Kodokan, my mother asked Kano sensei to find someone to marry me. But because Kano sensei suddenly died, I assumed any marriage plans died too. However, he had already talked about the request to Noriko Watanuki, who was his daughter and also the head manager of the women's department. And I realized that she took over my marriage issue for me.

One day, my mother and I were called to see the head manager of the women's department. My mother took me there assuming that she would talk about a marriage meeting. Then, before the manager talked about what the candidate was like, she abruptly asked me, "You do want to marry, don't you?"

I guess because I had a point-blank question, I frankly answered, "No. I'd like to do judo."

Then she said, "You don't intend to marry, do you?"

"No, I don't." The words spontaneously came out of my mouth.

"Then you won't marry, will you?" she said to me [gently laughing].

After the meeting, when I came back to the Kodokan and told everything about the conversation to the master Kiichiro Saeki, he simply said, "Fukuda, you can marry anytime if you meet a suitable man. You don't have to worry about it." I thought, *Maybe so*, and my worry was dispelled. After that, I thought only about judo every day. I was so relieved because I didn't have to think about marriage and marriage meetings.

Looking back now, answering, "I'd like to do judo," determined my life. I'm certain that my decision at that time was the starting point of who I am now.

I think I already had the firm purpose that I would become independent doing judo. I didn't talk about my idea with anyone in particular because it was my own idea. Even if I had talked about it to my mother or my brother, they wouldn't be able to change my mind or say anything.

Unlike the old days, now female judo athletes can continue judo after they have babies. Do you know a small-sized judo athlete called Yawara-chan? She has been doing a good job even after she had a baby. If you are small sized, you will fail unless you move very fast and are very strong. She might have an extreme talent. Thinking about female athletes like her, I think the women's judo world has changed very much. Compared to the past, the circumstances have remarkably progressed, and nobody has difficulties to practice judo. I hope people devote themselves to the practice as much as possible.

Kano sensei used to tell us, "I hope my female students go abroad and spread Japanese judo," and I also hoped to teach judo abroad, following his heart as well as his words. So I learned English conversation with an American instructor before the war. However, English became the enemy language.

My best friend, Ms. Tanaka, went back to Hawaii when the war started after Japan attacked Pearl Harbor on December 8 (according to the Japanese calendar, which is December 7 in the United States) in Showa 16th (1941). The war against America stopped news from her for a long time.

My brother wasn't inducted into the army because he was physically weak. I gradually heard that my friends went to see their brothers in training camps every week because their brothers even volunteered for special attack corps. My family lived as usual for a while, but my brother finally got a call-up paper in the final phase of the war.

Our family became all women, plus my brother's little boys. My mother, my sister, and I made an air-raid shelter, planted potatoes on a renting land in Ikuta (Kanagawa prefecture), and somehow managed to weather our life. The biggest difficulty was to have enough food in such a food-shortage era.

I went to the Kodokan every day even during the war. As air raids became more and more violent in Tokyo, half of the area around Suidobashi, where the Kodokan was, was burned. In spite of that, I went to the Kodokan from my house in Noborito. It was from my personal feeling that I would practice hard every day, as I had promised Kano sensei more than any obligation that I should protect the Kodokan.

I took a train as far as I could and then walked. Although I saw many burning houses, I wasn't so frightened. The most frightening was the B-29, because I would die if a bomb hit me. I quickly hid in a potato field if I noticed they seemed to be flying above me. I prepared vegetable soup for other students on a cold day, with the help of another student who held the second dan. Because there was no meat—it was so extravagant—I made the soup with daikon radish, greens, and so on.

In the meantime, students in the women's department evacuated from Tokyo. Noritomi sensei left for Fukuoka, and Atsuko Futaboshi left for her parents' home in the Kansai area. Only I remained to teach some students.

Yoshimaro Handa sensei, who was Kano sensei's favorite student, taught male students until the very end of the war. I think he felt indebted to Kano sensei very much. He said that he came to the Kodokan to see him every day, and he always bowed to a photograph of Kano sensei when he went home.

During the Tokyo air raid on March 10 in Showa 20th (1945), the houses that the Fukuda family rented out in the Kyobashi area were all burned down. We were just lucky that all my family members were alive.

The war finally finished in August in Showa 20th.

The GHQ of the allied Forces banned any Japanese martial arts as "military techniques." Of course judo was not excepted.

The Kodokan often explained to the GHQ that judo wasn't the skills to fight but a humanitarian sport intended to train the human mind. Eventually it developed that judo would be able to be taught in schools from Showa 25th (1950). Then American soldiers and judo athletes from all over the world came to the Kodokan to learn judo. I also went to the American army camp in Zama and taught judo in order to dispel the misunderstandings that Americans had.

Thank God that I socialized with American soldiers and their families more than anything else. I was glad that I could reconnect with Ms. Tanaka in Hawaii, who had been out of contact with me. After the war, when we were running short of supplies, she sent us different things. It helped us very much.

Thanks to the director's discretion, I trained under Kyuzo Mifune, tenth-dan master, for three years, after which I achieved fourth dan in Showa 21st (1946). Mr. Mifune was smaller sized than average, shorter than 160 cm (about 5.2 feet); however, he quickly threw larger people by skillfully breaking their balance. His throwing technique became famous as "an air throwing." Due to his height, he worked hard to think up new techniques, one after another. Nobody matched his achievements.

I was also thrown by him, and my body hit against the mats many times. The better I could do Ukemi, a defensive fall, the safer it became when I was thrown and the better I understood Riai, the theory.

As the social viewpoint toward women dramatically changed after the war, the Kodokan adopted the demand for more classes for women. The Kodokan that had previously taught only upper-class women opened the door of the women's department, set cheaper tuitions, and accepted everybody.

I also think that judo is the best sport for women because they become stronger, accomplish the art of self-defense, and cultivate their minds.

Jiro Nango, a former navy rear admiral, took over as manager of the Kodokan. He thought that women had to be skilled in the art of self-defense, and he started researching it with Shuichi Nagaoka, an instructor who held tenth dan, Kiichiro Saeki, and Kyuzo Mifune.

Noritomi sensei and I observed their work as we sat in the corner of the dojo. I learned greatly from the research by these eminent masters.

──────────────────── **From Umeko to Keiko** ─

Japan finally underwent reconstruction at the beginning of 1950, and the social atmosphere changed greatly. Due to that, the Kodokan became crowded with many students. I continued both training and teaching judo without worry because nobody said this and that about my marriage. However, because my pay from the Kodokan was low, and the house that my father left me as an in heritance had burned down, I was unable to provide for myself. So I lived in my parents' home into my forties. Thanks to that, I could only do judo [gently laughing].

At that time, my mother had a lengthy illness, and I took care of her except when I went to the Kodokan. Because she wasn't improving, one day I went to see a fortune-teller, whom a cook at the Fukuda Inn had recommended. After I explained my mother's condition, she said, "You will prove to be a failure if you keep your name." Several days later, she sent me a letter that said, "Change your name to 'Keiko Fukuda.' Don't use 'Umeko Fukuda' anymore." So I asked my family and employees to "Please call me Keiko." My brother's children were the only ones who didn't follow my request and still called me Auntie Umeko. Gradually all others called me Keiko.

Looking back now, changing my name might be related to judo. Strange to say, I had a lot of chances to go abroad as soon as I changed my name from Umeko Fukuda to Keiko Fukuda. The most important opportunity came in the form of a formal invitation to go to California.

The Kodokan manager said to three of us (Noritomi sensei, Ms. Mitsuboshi, and me), "An American lady will bring her students from America to the Kodokan. I need three of you to teach them." She was Helen Carollo, who is from California.

When she went back to America after having our training for half a year, Helen said, "Please, please come to America and teach judo." Perhaps she said it because her husband had a dojo. She had already bought a ship ticket for me. Because I was taking private English lessons with an instructor who had graduated from the Tsuda

English School (what is now Tsuda-juku University), I could speak broken English. I think that's why I was recommended.

I've never hesitated to plunge into unknown worlds and to start new things, ever since I was a child. I wasn't resistant to go to America, because foreign students came to the Kodokan to practice judo before the war, and I was close with my friend who was from Hawaii.

I heard the salary would be fifty dollars (18,000 yen at the then rate). I didn't think the amount of money mattered because I would live with Helen's family.

When I said, "They will give me fifty dollars," to my manager, he readily said, "I see. Take care of yourself. See you." When I asked my brother's opinion at home, he said, "You will learn something if you go abroad. Try it. If you need money, I'll send it to you. Don't worry." Because of his encouragement, I could easily make the decision.

Since it hadn't been long since the war ended in Showa 28th (1953), not so many people went to America. It was so rare for a woman to go to America by herself that a newspaper wrote about me.

I left Yokohama by a cargo ship for Seattle on the West Coast. When it left the wharf, many paper streamers were dancing and scudding on the wind. And then small boats chased after the streamers. Everybody, whether on the ship or seeing people off, cried at the sight. I was emotional too.

I wasn't worried about the two-week voyage because I could swim [gently laughing]! You must learn everything.

There were only two women on board: another woman who was going to America to learn piano and me. You may think a cargo ship is shabby; however, the captain considered our situation and gave us good service. It was very comfortable because we had meals with the upper-class passengers. It took about two weeks to Seattle, but I wasn't bored at all. I wasn't looking at the sea all the time, though. I don't remember in detail how I spent that time.

Don Carollo, Helen's husband, had his dojo in Oakland across the bay from San Francisco. Helen's father, a Japanese American from Hawaii, also taught judo there and had sent her to Japan to learn judo.

Back then in America in the 1950s, unlike now, women's social progress wasn't going so well. Almost all women became housewives, as Japanese women did. Helen was also mainly a housewife but taught judo in her spare time.

They made spaghetti whenever they had parties because they were an Italian American family.

They had two children. In the summer, they went to their second house in the mountains, at Christmastime they had parties, and on weekends they went driving and picnicking. They respected and treated me very kindly, inviting me to lots of events, making clothes for me, and so on. Thanks to them, I enjoyed American life very much.

American judo wasn't developed then, and instructors' level was low. One day as I observed a judo class in a nursery school, an instructor threw a child using a piggyback technique. I thought it was very dangerous; knowledge about judo was lacking. Nobody taught that judo is for character building, and almost nobody knew ju-no-kata.

So, many instructors wanted to learn judo handed down directly from the Kodokan in Japan and had a strong desire to learn new things. I was so happy because everyone was enthusiastic in the dojos and schools.

I taught as hard as I could. Because the Kodokan in Japan was still a special sanctuary of judo, the techniques were entirely different, including groundwork techniques and standing techniques. American instructors seemed impressed by experiencing judo of the Kodokan. When I taught ju-no-kata, everyone was glad and came to learn.

Even though I couldn't speak English well, I think I did a very good job. My English was so awful that the second-generation and the third-generation Japanese told me, "Sensei, please don't speak such English." But come to think of it, although they knew my English was poor, they respected my teaching and paid close attention to it. I appreciated them.

Before I left for America, an athlete who had more experience than me said to me, "Then stop acting as a referee anymore."

Although I didn't quite understand what it meant, I felt I had grown older. That memory led me to ask somebody when I was in America, "If I get older, I can't teach judo in other countries, can I?"

He said, "You have judo knowledge, don't you?" It was the very first time for me to hear such a thing, so I was stunned. If I were in Japan, people, especially women, were judged by age. However, in this country, if I had teaching techniques, people would value me no matter how old I was. I gained self-confidence when I understood that both men and women would be equally evaluated as judo instructors if they had knowledge. I think the experience led to my decision to continue judo in America.

At times I went from San Francisco south to San Jose. Carollo sensei and his wife took me to see their friends who taught judo there, and I met a lot of second-generation Japanese judo athletes.

Yoshihiro Uchida, who taught judo at San Jose State University, said, "It would be wonderful if we could teach Japanese culture through judo in order to wipe away the image of the defeated country." I agreed with his idea.

Since it hadn't been long since the war ended, there were misunderstandings about Japan and the Japanese, and also there were few Americans who could understand that our traditional culture was excellent. I thought it was worth teaching judo if people might become more respectful toward Japan and the Japanese through judo.

I had intended to go back after six months, but I enjoyed the teaching so much that before I knew it, it had been a full year. I could have stayed longer, but it might have become difficult for them to keep paying me. Also the Kodokan manager had simply encouraged me to "go for a good lesson." It was time to go home.

On the way back, I could visit Hawaii and see members of Yudanshakai, the dan holders' association. I knew that my good friend Ms. Tanaka was teaching judo there, and I stayed at her house! I was so glad that I could see her again. She and I remained best friends until she passed away.

I visited Canada too, besides Hawaii. When I arrived in Japan, it had been a year and three months. The teachers of the Kodokan teased me because I had become Americanized, wearing earrings.

--- **Tokyo Olympics** ---

After the war, the women's department of the Kodokan changed so that every woman could be a student; however, women were still banned from matches. Only men's judo was officially added to the Tokyo Olympic in Showa 39th (1964). Women's judo wasn't added until the Barcelona Olympics in Heisei 4th (1992).

Even though Noritomi sensei and I were chosen to demonstrate judo techniques for guests from abroad, the women's judo wasn't added to the official Olympics. We teamed up with each other and demonstrated ju-no-kata as usual. Kano sensei had always told us, "If ju-no-kata were grammar lessons, then randori, throwing and being thrown, would be composition lessons." If you don't master grammar, you can't make a beautiful composition. Thus, in judo, if you didn't learn a lot of positions, you would never be able to adapt many other offensive and defensive techniques. Because the foundation of judo techniques is positions, you will truly understand about judo spirit only when you master them.

It was a wonderful experience for me to demonstrate in front of a large gathering in the Japan Budokan in Kitanomaru Park, but for some reason, I don't remember that very much. I don't even remember if I was nervous or if my heart was pounding. I just remember that a teacher who held eighth dan demonstrated after we did. From behind, he had heavy legs. I remember I thought that a man like him was strong [gently laughing].

Noritomi sensei demonstrated as Tori, throwing, and I as Uke, accepting. This picture introduces a technique, Ryotedori. Knowing the photographs would be taken, we practiced every day for months, so we could demonstrate as usual. I didn't think I had done special things. I was just happy that it became an opportunity for people to know the world of women's judo.

I was filled with deep emotion about the Tokyo Olympics when I recalled that Kano sensei had enthusiastically guided Tokyo's campaign to host the Olympics before he passed away. The 1940 games were called off due to the war.

Keiko with the Olympic team

Keiko at 1964 Tokyo Olympics demonstration

FOUR

My New Life

ALTHOUGH I HAVE CITIZENSHIP AND teach judo in America now, I can't help thinking that the way that I got to this point was naturally determined. I'm sure that it is related to the fact that I was born as a granddaughter of Hachinosuke Fukuda, who was a jujitsu master. It is one of my reasons that strongly influenced me to continue judo for a long time.

Again, I never thought I would stay abroad for a long time. Probably I was thinking I'd stay for a year or so, because my mother was still alive in Japan.

The invitation for my second visit to America was exactly ten years after I came back from Oakland. A chairperson of the women's judo department of Yudanshakai, a dan holders' association, her name was Betty Wolfe, nominated me. It might be related to the fact that I had taught her before.

Again, I just naturally accepted the invitation, thinking, *If somebody invites me, I go*, at that time. I am not a person who asks,

"Please be sure to invite me." I am a person who just replies, "I see," if somebody says, "Please come." Because I taught very hard, although I was not social but reserved, people from different countries invited me.

I taught judo in many countries and visited many places I probably could not have visited otherwise. I appreciate Jigoro Kano sensei's teaching, which I always keep in mind, because it gave me the opportunity for such wonderful experiences. I'm not talkative; I can't even speak English very well. Not very attractive for foreigners, am I? However, I made a lot of friends all over the world through judo. I also appreciate that everyone accepted me the way I was.

When I came to America the second time, it was April 12 in 1966 (Showa 41st). I arrived in San Francisco right on my fifty-third birthday.

I didn't have much luggage, only judo uniforms and everyday clothes. Yes, I brought kimonos then. I specially ordered my kimonos because a famous actress whom I knew through the Kodokan recommended her favorite kimono shop for my visit to America. Thanks to her, people were excited to see me when I wore a kimono in California and in New York. For the life of me, I can't remember her name now. What was her name? A famous movie actress whose boyfriend was in America …

As soon as I arrived in San Francisco, I started teaching judo at dojos and schools, staying at different judo athletes' homes in different places.

When I taught at a dojo in San Francisco, I met Shelley. Oh, did I tell this story?

Although she was a beginner, she had a very good talent for judo. I recommended to her to participate in the summer practice at the Kodokan in Japan and to get the brown belt (from the third grade to the first grade).

The summer practice at the Kodokan, the same as the winter practice there, is a kind of discipline and training of the spirit, so students practice from 1:00 p.m. to 3:00 p.m., the hottest time, in the basement for ten days in a row. It is very hard even for the Japanese, so it is extremely hard for foreigners. However, once they get used to it, they develop wonderful stamina. More, they gain the strength of mind to achieve their goals.

Shelley did a good job and came back promoted to a higher rank. During her stay, she lived in the Fukuda Inn, my home in Noborito, and went to the Kodokan. Looking at her photographs, she was dancing wearing *yukata*, a cotton kimono, at a local Obon festival! I know she enjoyed living in japan.

After that, I think, Mills College in Oakland, from which Shelley graduated and was connected to, officially invited me, and I demonstrated different techniques. Those included the art of self-defense to protect yourself from a hoodlum with a gun or a knife. I also demonstrated randori, free exercises in judo, with a thickset man from Samoa, and ju-no-kata with Shelley.

As soon as I finished those, they asked me to teach judo for students at the school. I can't forget that Marie Nogues, the chairwoman of the Physical Education Department, said, "If you can teach Shelley, you can teach everyone." However, to become a regular teacher of the university, my green card that I received in 1967 (Showa 42nd) wasn't enough; citizenship was required.

— Accepted by America —

As you know, American citizenship is not easy to attain. I heard that it was difficult, especially for Asian people because there was a limit on the number accepted and the qualifications were strict. So

Shelley tried coming up with various ideas in that regard, developed a strategy, and negotiated with the immigration office for me. Thanks to her, I finally got my American citizenship in 1972 (Showa 47th). I was glad and relieved because I could teach judo without any inconvenience then. Thanks to my citizenship, I also started teaching judo officially at City College of San Francisco (CCSF). I think I was hired because a daughter of the chief priest at Sokoji, a temple that used to rent me its dojo, introduced me to Tanako Hagiwara, who was a physical education instructor there. When I taught the art of self-defense to students, the college officials observed it and recommended that physical education teachers also learn it. In that time, still not so many people in America knew judo.

I don't remember how much I received as a salary then; I have never cared much about money. I would have accepted whatever was offered. I think my environment while I grew up made my personality like this. Children in the Fukuda family grew up without knowing how to make money, but we grew old just the same.

Thanks to my citizenship, I was asked to teach judo at different universities and dojos in different states, so I visited, for example, New York and other cities near the Canadian border. It was not easy to visit many places, because America was a big country. While I was teaching judo in different places, time passed just like that.

In one year, I became confident that I could survive even with my broken English. When I demonstrated techniques directly transmitted from the Kodokan and talked about judo spirit, everybody enjoyed it in every dojo, club, and institute. It made me think about staying here and teaching judo longer. Then Shelley told me, "If it's all right, please live in my home and teach judo." I was so grateful to hear that because I wouldn't be able to support myself in Japan. Thinking about my future, America was the only choice for me.

I finally taught judo at CCSF for eleven years and at Mills College until my retirement at sixty-five.

I studied English harder than I do now. It was inconvenient if I couldn't speak English well, so I read newspapers, underlined words that I didn't know with a red pen, checked the words with a dictionary, copied them in my notebooks, and looked at them again and again. I did my best, but it didn't prove very successful. Now Japanese words come out from my mouth more than English. It bothers me.

Keiko's handwriting, learning English

After I retired from Mills College, I went to teach everywhere if somebody called me. I was so healthy that I visited my friends and took trips all over the world. I have been to Australia five times, France twice for judo seminars, Israel, Mexico, Canada, Norway, and so on.

When I taught at a seminar in France, I was past seventy-nine years old. I felt that maybe they were thinking, *What can an eighty-year-old woman do?* I didn't appear to be a judo master, because I was at that age and shorter than 150 centimeters (under five feet). However, after I demonstrated about forty throwing techniques, the image of being an old woman had disappeared. When I was invited by Sensei Pierre LeCaer, who has a dojo in Paris, three years later, I had a lot of students, including both children and adults. I appreciate that I still have been receiving Christmas cards and marrons glacés from people whom I met in many dojos in France.

It was interesting why I went to Norway with Sensei Freedman from Belize in 1989 (Heisei 1st). It was when I was teaching at my dojo in California. When I started the lesson, a stranger came and asked me to allow him to observe. Not only that; he said, "My whole family will go out today. Why don't you join us and have dinner at a restaurant after the lesson?"

I quickly answered, "It sounds good. Let's go when the lesson finishes," without knowing what was going on.

After the lesson, Shelley and I followed them and had dinner at a nice restaurant. During the dinner, he and I talked only about judo. After listening to him carefully, I knew he was a judo instructor. He said, "I go to Norway to teach every summer. Why don't you come with me?"

I said, "It sounds good."

When I arrived at the Oslo Airport, there was no one who had black hair like me. People walking past each other looked back at me because everybody had blond hair.

I taught ju-no-kata and randori at dojos and clubs where the instructor introduced me. It was a great trip because people were very kind to me wherever I went. It is interesting that I went to Norway by invitation from a person whom I didn't know at all [gently laughing]. It was a curious turn of fate or the course of nature.

People who met me in Norway came to visit San Francisco as an interchange group several years later, and we still keep in touch with each other. My trips seem different from others', don't they?

I also have a long good relationship with Patricia Harrington, a judo master in Australia. I had taught her in Japan when I taught at the Kodokan. I taught her very hard, so she might talk about me to the Australian Judo Federation.

The president of the federation invited me in 1965 (Showa 40th), and I went there to teach. I was amazed that Patricia's family living in Melbourne was so kind to me. Her mother learned how to cook Japanese food and cooked and served for me.

When I had judo sessions at the YWCA in Sydney, a lot of people not only from the club but also from other clubs gathered. When I went into the women's dressing room, a young woman quickly stood up and beautifully bowed to me. I felt as if I were back in the Kodokan in Japan. Although almost all the students were beginners, they waited for me sitting properly in Japanese fashion. I was so glad and amazed to realize that judo was preferred by people in a country far from Japan, as Kano sensei had wished.

Although I went to many countries for trips and teaching after my retirement from Mills College, I've hardly ever gone back to Japan since my mother passed away.

— Ju-no-kata —

I would like to talk a little bit more about ju-no-kata that I have been devoting my life to investigating. Can I? As Kano sensei said that ju-no-kata was like grammar, it is very basic and important. Each kata has a combination of techniques (Waza) by choosing typical movements, such as Kuzushi, Karada-sabaki (defensive body movement), and the way of using force, because judo techniques are based on rational thoughts. Nobody can accomplish ju-no-kata until he/she can surely do randori like a person who has a black belt. Ju-no-kata means never resisting against the other person. It is easy to say, but nobody can do it easily. A person who practices kata has to be physically and mentally flexible. In addition, a person who takes part in a match must be mentally strong. It is extremely difficult to keep good balance between both aspects. I rarely find a person who is good with both kata and matches. So ju-no-kata has to be absorbed by practicing again and again. Traditional judo had beauty of techniques because kata was more respected. Whenever you throw and are thrown by the other person, it is beautiful. But if you do it with all your strength, no beauty appears. I have just reached the point of understanding it after pursuing it for a lifetime. I am so happy to be able to fully follow the path of ju-no-kata.

I published *Born for the Mat*, the textbook of ju-no-kata, in 1973 (Showa 48th). I collected explanations of kata and, of course, the history and spirit of judo in the book for people who did not have the chance to go to the Kodokan and practice. I did my best, but it was very hard because I had never written a book. I could complete the book only with the support of many people who transferred video of kata into photographs and added English explanations. The textbook allowed me to teach at judo clubs, dojos, and schools in different places in America.

I started athletic competitions of ju-no-kata. I have been devoting myself to spreading of kata through them because it is related to training the mind. I am so glad to see that the number of people who practice kata increases year after year in America and in Japan and that the number of instructors has grown too.

Three or four years ago, I demonstrated kata at a judo meet in Canada. I could do it then. Wilina Monar sensei, one of my students who is from Hong Kong, did Uke for the demonstration. I heard that a local newspaper praised us.

Now a seventh dan teaches instead of me in various places in America. She started judo when she was thirteen years old and came to America when she was twenty years old. She is married to an American. She also has sixth dan by the Kodokan and the seventh dan here. She is an instructor who teaches kata with great energy and enthusiasm.

Another student holding fifth dan also demonstrates kata very beautifully. After I taught her, from the throwing technique to all the rest, she has reached such a point. The ju-no-kata that I have been teaching is transmitted directly from Kano sensei. I am proud of myself about this part.

— Seiryoku Zenyō, Jita Kyōei —

Kano sensei's teaching is condensed into the words, "Seiryoku Zenyō, Jita Kyōei." At the Kodokan, he often wrote the eight Chinese characters on a square piece of high-quality paperboard and explained the words as the moral philosophy of judo.

"Seiryoku Zenyō" is the use of one's mind and energy in the best condition. Maximum efficient use of energy by making mind and body one: that is judo. "Jita Kyōei" is harmony and cooperation of one's mind with others and society. Kano sensei taught us the right way of life to live cooperating with others, maximum efficient use of energy of mind and body.

After Kano sensei died, the following director (Jiro Nango, previously a Japan Navy rear admiral) also talked about the words again and again. There were some students who lacked spirit and said, "It has begun again." I tried to think, *Their learning styles are different from mine*, but honestly I was shocked. I guess some students died before they understood the judo spirit that Kano sensei taught.

"Seiryoku Zenyō, Jita Kyōei" is the essence of judo, so that Director Nango taught the words to us not only once or twice but again and again. If students always listened to it seriously, they would understand. "Oh, this is what Kano sensei tried to teach us."

I, myself, have practiced hard keeping what Kano sensei taught in my mind. I wrote the essence of "Seiryoku Zenyō, Jita Kyōei" in my book, and I often teach my students the essence of the words. The important thing is training of mind.

Some people asked me if foreign students could understand such things. I thing it depends on instructors. It is difficult because it is difficult for even Japanese people to understand. When I teach, I pick topics matching each student's lifestyle. Some students have told me that they had never listened to such spiritual talk in sports.

Once they understand that judo trains mind and body, they, including men, tell me, "I was wrong that I thought I had only to become strong physically."

FIVE

Be Strong, Be Gentle, Be Beautiful

My motto is "Be strong, be gentle, be beautiful," so I write this whenever I am asked to write something. This came to me relatively early in my training.

"Be strong" contains the meaning of strong will and strong body, both of which are necessary for judo. I think this is related to all kinds of martial arts. "Be gentle" comes from the word *ju*, which means soft or gentle. "Ju" contains very deep meanings. In the manual the Kodokan published in its early years, there is a picture of a small kimono-clad woman pushing a big man's chest. If she pushed his abdomen, he wouldn't move at all; however, he falls if she lightly pushes his chest. There are clear reasons. This is "Soft methods often get the better of brute force," the foundation of judo.

When I had the first practice with Kyuzo Mifune sensei, who is famous for "an air throwing," his grip on my uniform was so gentle that I didn't notice it at all. But as soon as I tried to throw him during randori, my body was flying in the air. I clearly remember the gentle feeling even now. My "be gentle" is not just being gentle but also being mentally strong.

"Be beautiful" doesn't mean a beautiful appearance but a beautiful heart; for example, consideration and kindness for others, and good will that takes the initiative to help people in trouble. The inner beauty is very important, and it is necessary for well-being. Although a lot of women are often swayed by appearances, they shouldn't forget beauty of heart. I added this in my motto because I wanted to always try to be a person whose heart was beautiful. I like it myself.

When I started practicing judo, people generally thought judo was for men. A lot of parents didn't want their daughters to practice judo. Judo was thought as a part of Bujutu, the martial art for the samurai. The reason why women's judo was accepted in America, Canada, Australia, the Philippines, and countries in Europe might be that people there didn't have such traditional ideas. I heard that lately in Japan, female judo athletes are more successful than male judo athletes. As I had thought, women are probably mentally stronger than men. Since mental strength is very important in judo, a person who knows it can win. When I see successful athletes, I can see how hard they have practiced to reach that level.

What Jigoro Kano sensei expected for women's judo was, I think, profundity and spirituality. I heard that Kano sensei said to male judo athletes, "If you want to understand judo more deeply, learn the methodology of women's judo." I think Kano sensei tried to find out the primary meaning of judo in women's judo in which the physical power is weaker and the physique is smaller. I have spent my whole life to find the heart of judo. Mastering the way of judo may be like being spiritually awakened in Zen Buddhism.

I learned a lot from Mifune sensei, especially that only when maximum efficient use of energy makes mind and body one, the wonderful technique will be born. The instant changes from movement to stillness and from stillness to movement can be caught only by the physical sense. If students want to get the sense, they have to practice the same techniques again and again until the body remembers the sense. They have to practice thinking why the positions became such.

By learning from Mifune sensei, I finally understand the scientific theory, including physical handling and necessity of confidence to develop the dignity of technique. I was deeply moved when I understood that science and philosophy were so embedded in the sport of judo. I thought, again, that judo was so profound. So I hope students practice ju-no-kata faithfully. The practices that I did at the Kodokan when I was young might not satisfy students who compete in matches, but they are very good for the spiritual training.

Japanese judo seems sleeping from where I live. One of the reasons is not so many people do training based on the teaching by Kano sensei. Not so many people research, present what they researched, and practice it. It is necessary to present the research, renew it, and let people know. For me, who practiced directly from Kano sensei from the beginning, his teachings nourished my body and soul. Even for a person like me, I don't have enough time to research the heart of judo through to the end. I think I need to train all my life.

— A Natural Posture —

I have had different experiences in my almost hundred-year life, especially physical changes. Although my body is mine, it seems it no longer belongs to me. It is a pity. I am giving people trouble when they pull me, hold my arms, and push me up because my legs don't move as I want them to. Are they kind to me because they respect judo? I wonder why my legs don't move well, but everybody who gets old probably becomes like me and needs others' help. I let it take its own course.

When I started judo, I was thrown once and had my backbone cracked. Since then, I have been having a hard time with my backbone. After I moved to America, I hurt my big toes. American men and women are tall, and they weigh several times what I do. Big Americans may think, *Can such a small person do judo?* I used to be treated by people as if they thought nothing of me. Some people asked me, "Are you really a teacher?" [Gently laughed.] I'm short, am I not? I'm shorter than 150 cm (four foot eleven). Because everyone was taller than me, I rode on their backs. Sometimes people teased me by picking me up and carrying me. However, with my maximum effort, I threw those big people who were teasing me. I stood so firmly that my big toes became deformed. I had surgeries for them and still have supporters on them.

Even so, I appreciate that my body has worked very well for me. When I was seventy-eight years old, I had triple bypass heart surgery. Ten years later, when I was eighty-eight years old, I had a disease that made my hands shake (Parkinson's disease). Ten more years later when I was ninety-eight years old, I fell and passed out at home. At that time, I didn't remember anything. When I came around, I was in a hospital. Shelley came and took care of me. I was hospitalized for ten days and came back to my home after New Year's Day, so I couldn't have any ceremony or a party. Maybe because of that, I sometimes think like I didn't have a New Year's Day yet.

My hand shaking has disappeared lately without my noticing it.

When I said to my acupuncturist, Alex Feng (who is also judo sensei), that it had gone naturally, he said, "It's a miracle!" A miracle means a miracle, doesn't it? It's exaggerated, although my friends and doctors are surprised whenever I overcome diseases and injuries. I myself don't know what is happening to me.

I have already lived here for more than forty-five years with a lot of people's support for my life. The only thing that is disappointing is that I don't have a friend in my neighborhood who speaks Japanese. Since Mrs. Tanaka in Hawaii, who had been my best friend for longer than seventy years after we met at the women's department of the Kodokan, passed away in 2007 (Heisei 19th), I have missed her so much. My lower back sometimes hurts after breakfast. When things like this happen, it's hard. I understand that nobody understands how hard it is even if I explain it as well as I can; still, I think if I had a Japanese good friend near here, it would be comforting.

Although my lifestyle became American, because I'm Japanese, I will never be able to lose my Japanese lifestyle. I often unintentionally speak Japanese. I probably want to speak Japanese. It's tiring for my age to speak only English every day.

Since I was born in Taisho period (1912–1926 CE), I am a person with old ideas. I sometimes comfort myself by listening to old Japanese songs and popular songs and playing a shamisen. I like a few old popular songs. I have a lot of Hibari Misora's music tapes. I still miss Japanese music. I remember Japan in the olden days whenever I play shamisen and listen to the music of my girlhood. At my age, I've been homesick for a lot of things. But I can't say I want to go back to Japan whenever I am homesick.

My nephew and his wife sometimes visit me from Hokkaido in Japan. Besides them, I can't see other relatives very often. I understand they are busy working. Thanks to the support of a lot of people, I was able to go back to Japan after a thirty-year absence. I stayed in Tokyo for ten days with Shelley and my students from America. During the visit, I observed the athletic meet of ju-no-kata and visited the Archives Center. I saw the displays of my grandfather, Hachinosuke Fukuda. I also appreciate that people arranged my lecture, so I had an opportunity to talk to many people about the teachings of Kano sensei.

I also visited my ancestors' graves at Kichijoji temple and cemetery, saw my school friends, visited the neighborhood of Kyobashi where I was born, walked around Ginza, and … what else? I really appreciate that people prepared everything, and everyone was attentive to the minutest details. I was surprised that Kyobashi was quite different from what it used to be. There were a lot of tall buildings, and there were no rows of houses that used to be common. Although I could not find anything related to my childhood, I experienced a sense of nostalgia. I visited Takashimaya, the department store, which was still there, and ate Japanese sweets at Yamamotoyama, a long-established tea store. It was as if I went back to my girlhood!

I was so glad that I could go back to Japan. I could not do that by myself at all! I thank Kaori Yamaguchi, a judo instructor at University of Tsukuba, and the people who made it possible. During my visit, everyone supported me thoroughly. The only thing to say is thank you. It was even more than thank you because I believed I could never go back to Japan.

There is a box on the family altar in the room over there with my posthumous Buddhist name inside. The chief priest at a Zen temple in downtown San Francisco prepared it for me in 1994 (Heisei 6th). Because I have been taken care of by the temple since I moved to San Francisco the first time, they know me very well. I didn't request what type of Buddhist name I'd like to have, nor what kind of Chinese characters I'd like to have in my posthumous Buddhist name. The priest said that it was decided naturally, as if it was given by Providence.

My posthumous Buddhist name is Shohoin Keioku Shudodaishi, which means that my soul will fly high up like "a bird that flies high up in the sky toward the sun and never die" [gently laughing]. He explained that to Shelley, so I think she also understands the meaning. I understand why she looked curiously at the name written with Chinese characters and in English, because most Americans don't fully understand about posthumous Buddhist names.

When I die, one half of my ashes are supposed to be buried in the Fukuda family's grave in Japan, and the other half is supposed to be buried with Shelley in Olivet Memorial Park in Colma as "Keiko Fukuda." I have already decided it. I said to Shelley, "Please take care of everything," if the time comes. Because I have my posthumous Buddhist name, she can hold my funeral anytime. With aging, I became concerned about such things in front of me because I am on the path to my death, aren't I?

Kano sensei's teaching is never far from my mind whether I do judo or not. I have been endeavoring to follow his teaching with all my strength. Looking back, my life has been happy. I'm not especially regretful or sad that I didn't marry and have a family. I don't wonder if it would be good if I had a child. There is no use in wondering because I didn't marry or have a child.

I had a lot of students since I established Soko Joshi Judo Club in 1967 (Showa 42nd). I was very busy, especially between the 1980s and the 2000s. The more students I had, the bigger dream I had that more people would know judo. That was when I began to think I would be able to follow Kano sensei's teaching.

I became the technical adviser of the women's judo department in the US Judo Association in 1967 (Showa 42nd) and became a referee in 1983 (Showa 58th). I also became the chief technical adviser of the association not only for women but also for men.

Lately, athletes wear white uniforms and light blue uniforms at international matches. The black belt for women used to have a white line, but it was banned because the US Judo Association ended the policy of separate designs for men and women. The idea of the uniform with colors, the black belt without classification of sex, and the changes of rules were adopted because of international ways of thinking. We can see from this how much judo has become an international sport. The more different ideas from different countries are introduced into judo, the more people say different things. I think it is natural that the rules and other things are adjusted.

In my dojo, on the other hand, we follow the practices and the promotions conforming to the Kodokan, so we have a white line on each black belt. I believe my students whom I gave black belts to will conform to the Kodokan, but who knows …

I hope to continue teaching from my heart because unfortunately women's judo in America is still developing. I hope female judo athletes continue practicing ju-no-kata and master it. It depends on individuals as to who and how many actually achieve dan. I always tell my students to keep in mind the training as humans. I hope I teach them that they will become helpful and broad-minded in any kind of society to which they belong.

Even so, I had never imagined that I would have such a life that I would spend so long a time without marriage in a foreign country. Even my grandfather Hachinosuke Fukuda might never have thought that I, his granddaughter, would continue judo for such a long time.

Recently, I had a dream that Hachinosuke was there. When I said to him, "It's about time for me to go where it is close to you," he said, "No. You still have to teach judo." He reproved me, saying this. So I hope I devote myself to the spreading of women's judo all over the world and hope a lot of people know more about judo from Kano sensei's words as long as I live. If I didn't, my grandfather won't forgive me! [Gently laughing.]

SIX

Fukuda Shihan

─ **Let People Respect the Japanese** ─

The following pages are recollections from a variety of people who knew Keiko.

YOSHIHIRO UCHIDA, HEAD COACH OF the judo team at San Jose State University, eighth dan from American Judo Association

When Fukuda shihan visited America for the first time in 1953 (Showa 28th), I was teaching judo at San Jose State University. When I heard that a judo instructor from the Kodokan in Japan would come to America, I wanted to see her. Moreover, I was excited that she had learned judo directly from Grand Master Jigoro Kano. Since my friend knew Mr. and Mrs. Carollo, who invited her to their dojo in Oakland, he arranged that we would meet each other at his house. I remember that we had Mexican food, and I did randori with her in the tatami room in his house. We were surprised at her nimble and quick movement and flexibility at age forty.

I also explained the situation for the Japanese in America. There were a lot of soldiers who came back from the World War II, and a lot of people still remembered the battle against Japan and President Roosevelt's Executive Order 9066, which excluded all persons of Japanese ancestry from the West Coast and put them in internment camps. In addition, the popular local exhibitions were matches between judo and boxing and judo and wrestling. When a judo athlete was thrown, people cheered as if they had defeated the Japanese. I remember that I said with hope, "It is a good time for us to apply judo to present proper information about the Japanese and Japanese culture."

While the martial art in America is that people aggressively fight each other, Japanese judo techniques are gentle. Its teaching is strict with the etiquette and the manner because it also has spiritual aspects. Americans who were interested in the "gentleness" of Japanese judo were fascinated by her ju-no-kata, which was her masterpiece. Moreover, she cared so much about safety that I've never heard that anybody was injured at her dojo. These are reasons why so many people have admired her Soko Joshi Judo Club.

She became a famous judo instructor because she bravely reached out to the American people and visited and taught judo in almost all the states in just one year. In addition to her contribution to American women's judo development, the gender equality movement in America matched well with it.

In 1972 (Showa 47th), Title IX, a comprehensive federal law that prohibits discrimination on the basis of sex in any federally funded education program or activity, was approved. This law of equality for both sexes changed women's sports so much that women could win sports scholarships and could become professional athletes. Gender equality had eventually been realized in the sports world. It can be said her contribution succeeded then because it swam with the tide.

Her tenth dan given from the USA Judo Association in 2011 (Heisei 23rd) followed by United States Judo Federation (USJF) was meaningful for her life, although it is my personal opinion that the Kodokan should have given her the tenth dan. They still hold old-fashioned views about women unfortunately.

Daniel Kikuchi, judo professor at San Jose Community Center

My first encounter with Fukuda shihan was when I watched her on television. She demonstrated ju-no-kata at the Tokyo Olympic Games in 1964 (Showa 39th). Although I was a child and didn't understand about judo, I remember that her demonstration was so beautiful and deeply impressive.

When I learned ju-no-kata from her, she strictly made me practice it again and again. When I tried to cut corners in my practice, she would stand up behind me before I knew it. Suddenly she scolded me with a strong voice saying, "Do it more seriously!" I, a boy back then, would shudder with fear. Relating to Title IX that Uchida shihan mentioned before, she fulfilled the important mission to lift women's social status through judo. Unlike some activists who demanded gender equality and revolutions, she has achieved her mission in a softer way. Her ways were always moderate, but certainly she supported women's rights. This is one part of her greatness. Her teaching is limitless because judo training is connected with spiritual training. It covers how we can improve our world and adapt the samurai spirit to all human beings. Since she has the philosophy directly taught by the grand master Kano, she could spread judo even better in American society.

Eiko Saito Shepherd, chairwoman of kata in the USJF, sixth dan from the Kodokan and seventh dan from the USJF

After I studied judo for about two years, I started learning at the Kodokan in 1962 (Showa 37th). Since then, I have known Fukuda shihan. I remember she came to the dojo earlier and left there later than anyone even though she was already an instructor who held a higher dan.

When my elder brother participated in the Asian Games, he left home wearing his uniform. I, seeing him off, longed to be like him. This was why I started judo. Since women's competition was banned in Japan, I moved to America in 1966 (Showa 41st) out of my single-minded desire to compete, even though I couldn't speak English. Luckily, I could learn judo from her again.

Since she is very humble, she never told us about difficulties that she encountered. I know that she must have had a lot of hardships when she started teaching judo in America. For example, while she taught students to do kata properly again and again, both men who didn't know about judo and male judo athletes criticized her, saying, "Women do such practice because they can't compete in different countries." However, she never changed her mind but trusted herself that it was what she needed to teach. This is how she is. This is one part of her greatness. She has never been agitated by what other people said. I was deeply impressed when I heard she had remained calm even when people had severely criticized her in many different dojos. She is a real instructor. Her attitude is convincing. It reminds me the proverb, "If you strive, you achieve." Her great persuasiveness through her action stems from her dedication to living according to her beliefs and practicing them every day in her life.

For her tenth dan from the USA Judo Association and the USJF that she earned in 2011 (Showa 23rd), she never said that she would ask about the promotion. The grade for both Fukuda shihan and Noritomi sensei used to remain the fifth dan for thirty years. When the Kodokan offered Noritomi sensei the sixth dan, she asked for the seventh dan because she had also learned directly from Grand Master Kano and had taught at the Kodokan for a long time. However, Fukuda shihan never said things like that.

As a female judo athlete, I feel very sorry for her not to earn the tenth dan, the highest grade, even though she has devoted her life to judo until now, as she is nearly one hundred years old. In her winning the tenth dan from the USA Judo Association and SFJF, there is the message that women outside of Japan will be rewarded for their efforts. The message encourages us very much.

Frances Christy, chief editor of *United States Judo Federation JUDO* magazine

I am an editor of *United States Judo Federation JUDO* magazine for judo fans in the United States and a student of Fukuda shihan. How I started learning judo was that I noticed my body, mind, and spirit were not in balance because of work pressures. She didn't teach judo as a simple sport but has always talked to us about the spirituality in judo through her belief "be strong, be gentle, be beautiful." I don't know any sport but judo that even teaches how humans should live. She used to be a severe, strict teacher, but she became much gentler as she aged. She now naturally accepts physical support from people. It surprises me because I know how she used to be when she was strong and more physically active. If I have to describe her with one word, I would like to say that she is indomitable. I admire her for her determination to devote her life to judo. I think we have to follow her example.

Dr. Alex Feng, practitioner of acupuncture and judo instructor in Oakland, California

As a practitioner of acupuncture and judo, I have been in charge of management of Fukuda shihan's physical condition since the 1970s. However, I have never thought of her as my patient. I am more of her eternal student than she is my patient [gently laughing]. I respect her as my mentor and am honored to associate with her.

I, who specialized in Taoism, enjoy spending time with her, feeling as if I was embraced by her big, gentle love. It is very difficult to describe this feeling. We don't need much conversation to understand each other because our qi (energy flow) connects between us.

I believe that she moved to San Francisco guided by the greater power. In other words, she might have had no choice but to follow her destiny. In the given circumstances, she commendably became rooted and then bravely became in magnificent bloom. Everybody has been willing to support her because of receiving her judo knowledge, love, and kindness.

Is there any other woman like her? She is beyond cultures, common sense, and everything! Japanese people have to be more proud of her because she is not only a great judo athlete and a role model but also a woman.

Anne Thorson, MD, professor of cardiology at University of California, San Francisco

When Fukuda shihan was seventy-eight years old, she had triple bypass heart surgery. Two of the bypasses occluded, broke down. For her age, it was a serious surgery. Since then, I have been in charge of her periodic medical examination as her doctor. As a result, now she keeps in good condition physically and mentally for her age, ninety-nine years old. After the surgery, her heart condition miraculously improved so much that she doesn't have to worry. Her blood pressure and pulmonary functions are normal, and her skeletal system is steady too. Her knee pain and back pain are normal for her age.

Her good condition in her old age should be based on her physical and mental toughness, as she has trained for a long time. A person like her who is passionate about her mission, judo, and clearly determined goals is a model of well-being.

Dr. Shelley Fernandez, Keiko's life partner and joint owner of Soko Joshi Judo Club

I started learning judo with Fukuda shihan in 1966 (Showa 41st) when I was a judo student at Koyokan dojo in San Francisco. I had never seen such a quick, sharp, and concentrated judo. I was completely fascinated by her judo.

While learning judo, I also had a busy life as a women's rights activist. I served two terms on the national board of National Organization for Women (NOW) and was president of San Francisco NOW. I am the founder of La Casa de las Madres, the first shelter for battered women in the United States. I am also the founder of Our Lady of Guadalupe Health Center in San Mateo County, a free clinic for disadvantaged people funded by the federal government Health Education and Welfare (HEW). I have helped Fukuda shihan continue teaching judo since she arrived. I have offered her my house, opened her dojo, helped her find jobs and get her citizenship, appealed to the US Judo Federation and the federal government, and kept her in good health in order that she be able to think about only judo. I was responsible for sending a petition to the Kodokan with thousands of signatures requesting her promotion of the sixth dan after being the fifth dan for over thirty years. Dan promotion for men is every ten years.

A lot of people asked me why I helped her so much. The answer is very simple. She is a miracle worker. I'm not the only person who knows this. Everybody around her knows this too. I love her very deeply and am happy to give back to her as best I can because she has given so much of herself to me in so many ways.

Not only is her life force a miracle but also her determination to teach judo taught from Kano shihan. Her emotional strength, her personality that naturally calms others, and everything about her—it is all incredible. I seriously believe that God protects her. She is a Zen Buddhist and a member of Sokoji Zen temple in San Francisco. I believe that she is a real Bodhisattva that achieved satori, which means enlightenment here on earth. She is truly more than a master of judo. She is a master of life and kindness.

Her existence itself is a treasure for all of us. It surely is the same for the Japanese, isn't it? However, for a long time, the Kodokan didn't appreciate how much she has meant for judo just because she was a woman. I asked a person of high rank in the Kodokan who visited here years ago, "Why isn't she eligible to earn the ninth dan?" He answered promptly, "Because she is a woman." It didn't make sense because she was already so famous among judo athletes that Russian president Putin had asked her to write a foreword for his judo book in 2004 (Heisei 14th). I cannot forget that answer. I hope that soon the Kodokan will award her the tenth dan since America has already correctly done so. They should also provide space for her between her grandfather Hachinosuke Fukuda and Kano shihan in the Kodokan museum and library. She would be the woman so honored.

We had gathered signatures for her ninth dan in different places in America and asked the Kodokan to confer it for her, and then she finally earned the ninth dan from the Kodokan, following its regulations in 2006 (Heisei 18th). She earned the tenth dan from the USA Judo Association and USJF in 2011 (Heisei 23rd). America paid its respects for her earlier than Japan did. Needless to say, she was happy, but because of her humility, she didn't express publicly her deep happiness.

We called her "Sensei Keiko Fukuda," but since she is the first and only female tenth dan holder in the world, we are going to call her "shihan (grand master)." I believe that Fukuda shihan will teach and spread judo until her life ends and will continue showing the model of "the way of life of being a good human person."

Kaori Yamaguchi, associate professor of the Graduate School of Tsukuba University

Ms. Yamaguchi was born in Tokyo in Showa 39th (1964). The bronze medalist in the women's judo at the 1988 Seoul Olympic Games, 6th dan holder from the Kodokan. A director of the Japan Olympic Games Committee. She won four silver medals at the world championship, and she won the first gold medal for Japan judo team at the third championship in Showa 59th (1984). She retired in Heisei 1st (1989). While she teaches at the Graduate School of Tsukuba

University, she strives to spread judo by holding "Kids Judo," judo events for children all over Japan.

From birth, we have chance and necessity. Probably we have less chance than we expect. Generally speaking, children cannot choose their place to be born; however, they seem to be born with their own missions to be fulfilled during their lifetime. Considering Fukuda shihan's life, I can't stop thinking that she is a chosen person born of necessity to teach judo.

She was born as a granddaughter of Hachinosuke Fukuda, who was a jiujutsu master of Jigoro Kano. After Grand Master Kano built the Kodokan, he held a memorial service for his master, Hachinosuke Fukuda. When he visited the Fukuda family for an announcement about the ceremony, he invited her to try judo. It was the chance for her to start leaning judo. Considering the period, there probably were few families that encouraged their daughters to do judo. However, it's understandable because of her lineage. Her father died at an early age, and her brother was physically weak. Hachinosuke's wife might be glad that she succeeded the job that her husband had achieved even if her granddaughter was female. From what she has told me, her grandmother had a strong will at times, and that strong personality kept her to be able to support and manage her family. Her grandmother didn't deny her learning judo. It must have pushed Fukuda shihan to start.

However, now that I understand how she started judo, I still wonder what the true reason was. I have never heard that she was interested in sports or especially active. If anything, she grew up in rather comfortable circumstances and was an elegant woman who did Japanese calligraphy and Japanese traditional flower arrangement. Although times have changed, she's never insisted on expressing her opinions. On the other hand, she keeps the strong thoughts all to herself by exemplifying from the fact that she moved to America by herself. She might have felt something missing to follow the way laid out as a Japanese woman, although she's never said so.

To tell the truth, she had a formal meeting with a view to marriage. She declined it. At that time, it was extremely difficult to continue teaching judo after marriage because, traditionally, women became housewives. She might have decided to spend her whole life single-mindedly in judo being unmarried then. It is also possible to infer that she decided to move to America in her fifties due to critical viewpoints toward single, middle-aged women and difficulties of making a career for herself as a professional. After Grand Master Kano's death, the atmosphere in the Kodokan might have changed. No matter how hard she tried to teach according to his teaching philosophy, people evaluated female instructors poorly. There were limitations to what women could do. Eventually, she moved to America and extended her experiences. The details of how she achieved her mission of passing her master's will to others in America are explained in this book.

By the way, I would like to add what the Kodokan judo is and who Grand Master Kano was. He endeavored to spread sports in Japan. He founded the Kodokan in Meiji 15th (1882) and started the women's division in Meiji 26th (1893). In addition, he founded the Japan Amateur Athletic Association (the forerunner of Japan Olympic Games Association) and played an active part in the first Asian committee in the International Olympic Games. In the judo world, he devoted himself to teaching judo, putting stress on education, "development of humanity," and "being beneficial to the world."

On the other hand, he might have known that male judo competitors would become more physical than mental, as you see it now in the Olympic games. So, he might expect female judo players to take over his ideal of judo training by prohibiting women from matches at that time. In his later years, he said, "Women's judo is the real way." His words appear to me that the female judo contains his real intention that he sought and expected. In fact, he had put the women's division next to his office and would often teach his women students.

When I started learning judo at the Kodokan, the women's department was called "the ladies' chamber." He would strictly choose female students by interviewing them himself and gave them special education in order to train them as successors. Fukuda shihan must have been an honor student among them. She might see her father, who died early in his life, in Grand Master Kano. She still admires him and uses his words as if it is her Bible. I sometimes made a joke with other judo athletes, saying, "We believe in Kano-ism," as a metaphor that his teaching was an unconditional measure for us to think and follow. His words are still so influential, even for us who didn't directly learn from him, that those words must have been as the divine Word of God for students who directly learned from him.

You cannot control the outcome of judo matches. There is no guarantee that a person will win even if he or she followed his teaching. The male judo athletes, who competed, may just have a practical side even though they understand his ideal and theory. In contrast, the female judo athletes, who could not compete then, might have more closely followed his teaching.

I met Fukuda shihan at the first women's International Judo Championships in New York in 1980 (Showa 55th). Although I heard that she was a great instructor, I didn't know her very much. After that, I read an article in the newspaper that she had earned the first ninth dan for a woman from the Kodokan. Since I had been writing serial articles titled "History and problems in women's judo" in a martial art magazine, I was very interested in her. So, I visited San Francisco to talk to her. Although she was already ninety-four years old then, her way of talking was stable, and what she said was very interesting. Moreover, she went to her dojo three times a week. Eventually what I most remember when I left there for Japan was her statement, "I think 'there is Japan across the sea' whenever I see the sea." She unexpectedly said that as if confiding a secret when we drove to a restaurant for lunch. I am sure that she has no regret at devoting herself to judo; however, I am certain that she felt nostalgic about Japan as the years went by. I naturally said to her, "Please come back to Japan, sensei." This was the start of my project for her return to Japan. I gathered her airfare by calling and talking to many judo athletes, irrespective of sex or age. Then finally she came back to Japan for the first time in a couple of decades. Some people were wondering, "She is not close to Fukuda shihan. Why?" I met her only twice, to be sure, but I immediately related to her beyond reason or logic because of who she was. It was my great motivation to achieve the project.

The women's judo is now popular as an athletic competition. The status of female instructors was also elevated. For the London

Olympic Games in coming 2012 (Heisei 24th), the Japanese women's judo is expected to win more medals than the men's judo. I'm sure that judo will improve and spread more and more. That is why I think it is important for us to improve our judo based on the history of the women's judo and its role. We mustn't forget pioneers like her who laid the foundations for the present prosperity of the women's judo.

Not many people can live like her. However, everybody can learn from her. Her devoted life to judo is dignified and magnificent.

Navneet Gill, Keiko Fukuda's student and the originator of establishing women's judo in India

I'll forever be grateful for the series of little coincidences that brought Sensei into my life and gently, strongly, and beautifully changed it forever.

I had always been interested in martial arts, but while growing up in India, there wasn't any opportunity to learn.

Years later, after I moved to the United States, I studied with

Sensei. I met her when she was in her mid-nineties. For five years I had the opportunity to learn from her, not only about judo but also about strength, dignity, perseverance, and the indomitable will to work hard toward your goals.

She taught till the end. Her discipline and dedication were legendary. She was on the mat every single class. Even when she was in a wheelchair, she wouldn't miss a thing happening way in the back of the room; nothing got past her.

Her whole life was dedicated to judo. By the life she lived and the priceless gifts she taught, she became a living symbol of women's empowerment. She broke the glass ceiling in judo, and other forms of martial arts followed suit.

When she died, I realized how lucky I was to have met her and how imperative it was to spread her knowledge and spirit. I decided to use what I had learned from her to address the injustice that had always rankled—the inability of girls to walk down the streets of India without fear. Fear of being robbed, yelled at, eve-teased, molested, hit, abused.

With the help of Dr. Shelley Fernandez, who backed the proposal instantaneously and has given full support of the Dr. Shelley Fernandez and Shihan Keiko Fukuda Judo Foundation, I set out to explore the feasibility of teaching much-needed self-defense and judo to girls in my hometown of Patiala, India.

From giving demos on concrete floors to girls from the poorest backgrounds who had never even heard of judo (or any martial arts), we've become a program in its third year that has seven judo centers/dojos and has taught thousands of girls how to defend themselves.

All this would not have been possible without Mr. Sharma, head of NIS Judo, retired, and our chief adviser, Mr. Jiwan Sharma, head of NIS Judo, and our honorary and irreplaceable adviser, Mrs.

Divya Sharma, our adviser and chief coach, Sajida Channa, our head instructor, and all the coaches, students, and staff of NIS Patiala. Ms. Ramneet Jeji, a childhood friend, very graciously and ably is running the entire program in India, along with Navneet Jeji, Mrs. Gurmit Gill, and DC Varun Roojam.

We are now starting a partnership with the district authorities and expanding to more schools in partnership with the government's "save the girl child" movement. Our goal is to give access to judo and self-defense to every girl in every school in India.

It had seemed a very lofty aim three years ago, but then we had a very lofty example set for us that inspired us every step of the way. Sensei had always worked on finding a solution—gently but surely and strongly chipping away at the problem till she broke through. She had worked against so many odds, never giving up hope, and in the end achieving what she had set out to do. Her path hadn't been easy, but she had made a big difference in the end—one class at a time. Her memory, spirit, and example live on for thousands of girls to be inspired by. Her magic has touched these girls. They've not only learned judo and self-defense, they've gained confidence and hope for a better life.

Ramneet Jeji, coordinator / general secretary for the Shihan Keiko Fukuda Memorial for the promotion of judo for women in India

In the field of judo, Shihan Keiko Fukuda holds a special place as the only woman to have reached tenth dan. What better tribute to her than to keep her legacy alive by empowering young girls in self-defense through judo. With this view in mind, Dr. Shelley Fernandez, the president of the Keiko Fukuda & Shelley Fernandez Girls & Women Judo Foundation, Inc., decided to empower young girls in self-defense through judo in Patiala, India.

During my school days, I took judo training along with my friend Navneet Gill, who later trained under Sensei Fukuda in San Francisco. We trained under Sensei J. G. Sharma and Mr. Jiwan Sharma in Patiala at their dojo.

We knew going forward we would have Sensei Sharma's support and expertise. The response to the judo demonstrations that we organized was huge. School administrators also felt it was the need of the hour, keeping in mind how in today's time it is vital for everyone to know self-defense. It appealed to me because of its easy accessibility in schools, as while growing up we were never provided an opportunity to learn any martial arts in school. The girls are fortunate to have this training available to them in their respective institutes.

Initially, we did demonstrations at local schools and colleges, and on seeing the overwhelming enthusiasm, we started the training in April 2014. A small technique rightly administered, and you have the satisfaction of seeing your opponent lying flat on his back; it seemed easy, and girls wanted to learn. Early on, we conducted some classes in the open playing fields on the campus, owing to the unavailability of mats or a designated room. Seeing the enthusiasm of the learners, the school administrators did their part in helping set us up wherever they could.

Gradually, we reached out to more schools, providing them with mats as well as judo uniforms when required, as the students at the government-run schools belong to really poor backgrounds. Girls are taught by black belt women trainers and Sensei Sharma, who are members of the advisory board and design the curriculum for training. Girls have been taught that the key to mastering judo is correct technique and balance, not muscle or power.

The look of awe and disbelief on the girls' faces after having followed through with a correct technique is priceless. We have also been fortunate to have international experts generously volunteer their time to give training to girls. Geoff Malone, a fifth-degree black belt in jujitsu from San Francisco, visited Patiala in November 2014 for the sole purpose of instructing the girls, as did Sensei Alex Feng, a fourth-degree black belt in judo from San Francisco, and then Sensei Clara Sanchez, a third-degree black belt in judo from Spain, in November 2015. The interaction with these gifted teachers has inspired and motivated the girls and also given them an incentive that if they do well and practice, who knows—tomorrow one of them could be a champion.

In my interaction with the girls, I often see the spark of curiosity and the zest to learn more. Toward this end, the input of visiting teachers goes a long way to keep their interest alive.

The girls feel honored that they have been given this privilege. They go home and show off their newly acquired skills to their siblings and parents. As the training progresses, it is heartwarming to see the confidence that shines through in the girls' demeanor.

Beginning with just three schools/colleges in 2014, to nine in 2015, we are hopeful of starting the training at five more in 2016. On a rough estimate, some five hundred girls have received training, and double that number have attended the intensive workshops for self-defense.

My hope is that Shihan Fukuda's legacy to uplift these girls and mold them into better human beings—which is the essence of judo, to be gentle, to be kind, and to be beautiful inside and outside—through quality judo training will spread, and one day all girls in Patiala will know the basics of self-defense.

Special thanks to Dr. Shelley Fernandez for requesting and allowing me to write about Patiala so that it could be included here.

Isabel Wade, Keiko's student, inaugural judo class at Mills College, 1967

When I was in high school, a neighbor tossed me into the air to demonstrate his newfound judo skills. Consequently, when judo appeared on the roster of physical education classes for my sophomore year in college, my interest was piqued to see if I could learn the same magical skill. At this point, I assumed that judo was all about physical action.

The first of several surprises upon meeting Mills's first and only judo instructor, Keiko Fukuda, was her tiny size and her restrained and gentle manner. Clearly one did not have to be an amazon to become the best female judo player in the world. She also laughed a lot, and despite her lack of much English at that time, she managed to convey the mind-body aspect of judo and the importance of the complete package to both successful judo and the conduct of one's life. Her motto—be kind, be gentle, be beautiful—exemplified this mind-body connection.

While I did not continue my judo training past brown belt level (earned after my college years), I did continue my friendship with

Fukuda Sensei and enjoyed many years of warm visits and deep conversations with her. As I got to know Keiko more over the years, I could see that she really lived her mandate, and it drew many amazing people into her life. I tried to apply her precepts in my own life, although it is not always an easy task to be kind and gentle. But as a senior citizen now, I especially value the applications of kindness I observe or can participate in. And I think often of Keiko while considering that the planet could urgently use some gentle love too from all of us.

Koré Grate, Judo sensei and board member of the Shelley Fernandez and Keiko Fukuda Judo Foundation

On the day before I left Minneapolis to travel across the world, my little *Daily Meditation—365 Tao* book read: "You may be contemplating a very bold move in your life." No kidding, thanks to Dr. Shelley Fernandez, president of the Keiko Fukuda Judo Foundation.

This is the fourth year the nonprofit foundation has been offering classes for girls in judo and self-defense within the school systems of Patiala, India. The gang rape and death of twenty-three-year-old Jyoti Singh on December 16, 2012, triggered widespread media coverage, including the documentary *India's Daughter*, which created an opening for India to begin to shift the ancient attitude toward girls and women. The program honors Shihan Keiko Fukuda's legacy of "be strong, be gentle, be beautiful in body, mind, and spirit," and the girls are learning how to be all that and more. The first year started with demonstrations led by Navneet Gill, Raman Jeji, and Navneet Jeji, with the support of Sensei Jai Gopal Sharma, retired head coach of Judo-National Institute of Sports (NIS). By the second year, there were three schools committed to the program, one of which is the British Co-Ed High School and Principal Rose Kucharskyj, who transports girls from the outskirts of town (i.e., poverty level) to participate in classes. For those who don't know, this is a very rare occurrence in India. By the third year, there were nine schools, and this year there are twelve.

Sifu Sonya Richardson, head instructor of Hand to Hand Kajukenbo in Oakland, California, and I traveled for twenty-four hours with Dr. Shelley Fernandez, from San Francisco to Newark at 9:00 a.m. November 3, and landing in New Delhi on November 4 around 9:00 p.m. On November 5, Ashish, our driver, expertly navigated the six-hour northwest drive to our nonhotel, the Bara Dari Palace in Patiala in the Punjub district, our home for the next ten days.

After resting and cleaning up, we were invited to Raman and Navneet Jeji's home for a traditional Indian dinner by Mom! Truly a gift, the spices are both subtle and powerful—a form of art! Mr. and Mrs. Jeji, Navneet, and Dr. Shelley visited at home while Raman took Sonya and I sightseeing to the Punjab Museum, historical grounds that were part of her heritage, and shopping for traditional Indian shirts and scarves (kurtas and dupattas). We needed dressy clothes to attend important events. While we were teaching, we stayed in our uniforms the entire day, and we didn't bring much more than a few comfy articles to hang out in.

Monday, November 6, Sifu Sonya and I taught our first class of the Five Fingers of Self-Defense and Empowerment (Mind, Voice, Escape, Fight, and Tell) at the Government Senior Secondary School (GSSS) Old Police Line to girls in sixth and seventh grade. We were scheduled for one hour for each session. We were scheduled to teach in five schools per day for six days. Sometimes the hour turned into twenty minutes due to protocol of visiting the principal and having Marsala chai tea and cookies beforehand (having jet lag, the chai and sweets really helped us keep going!). After three days, we had taught all twelve of the classes enrolled in the foundation program. We were able to return to many of the schools to teach a second class to go over what they had learned and add a few more techniques. The girls ranged from six to twenty-five years old, and even though it is illegal now to talk about the caste system, we noticed that the girls from the "community program—bussed-in/untouchables" were the most appreciative of everything we taught and were deeply inspiring for us. We taught how to stand up tall, do a power pose, how to say "no" loudly, how to yell commands, how to escape grabs and chokes, how to throw someone who grabs your dupatta (traditional scarf won by all girls and women), how to do a hammer fist to someone on a scooter who pinches you from behind, how to strike vulnerable/soft targets with natural weapons, that it is okay to talk to someone you trust, to ask for help, and to not be ashamed that someone harmed you or tried to harm you. We did this all within an hour or less, which made us condense the material, especially when a lot of what we said had to be translated into Punjabi or Hindi or both. Then we were off to the next school, which was a fifteen to thirty-minute hair-raising drive amidst cows, scooters with five people astride (sometimes a baby), dogs, people walking across highways (at night too), no stoplights, no speed limits, and always driving into the "empty spaces," no matter which side of the road they were on.

Being a day ahead of the United States, we were also keeping track of the election, and ironically, the people from India were rooting for Trump. It was a very surreal experience to say the least, as on the day Trump won, the Indian rupee in 500 and 1,000 denominations were banned, taken out of circulation by Prime Minister Modi. The 500 and 1,000 rupees were the only denomination we were given by the exchange banks in the United States. That was a shocking day. We had a new president, and we were poor. Thanks to our host family, the Jejis, and our credit cards, we worked it out, but still, we came home with "monopoly money" that our banks won't exchange back.

On November 10, we were asked to have the high school girls from GSSS Multi-Purpose School demonstrate for the DC (district commissioner), which is like the mayor of the town and a big deal. We taught one class with these girls for less than an hour two days previous, and they were one of the newer additions to the foundation, with only one week of judo. Navneet Gill and Raman had a meeting with the DC to request support from the government to continue offering the classes in the coming year, as it is growing so fast, and the foundation is barely keeping up. The DC took time out of his busy schedule to come see for himself. As we waited for his entourage and escort to arrive, we quickly put together a demo of judo and self-defense techniques with Sensei Shallini, Sensei Suchicka, and Sensei Cuomo. We all worked together flawlessly, and when he arrived, the girls put on a twenty-minute perfect demo. He publically thanked us afterward and invited us to a special concert the following evening with Kanwar Grewal, who is a famous Sufi-ish chanting singer. I was enthralled by his voice and found out later that he was singing-chanting about protecting women and girls. We were all brought up and honored on stage with an award for the work the foundation is doing for girls. We had to leave early to attend yet another special invitation from Principal Rosa from the British School for an annual staff party. The night before, she had invited us as honored guests to attend Celebrating the 400th Anniversary of William Shakespeare—*Romeo and Juliet*. Can I just say that we definitely felt appreciated and that India has the best music, young theatre performers, and dancers and the most delicious food!

A highlight of our trip was the story of a young girl named Adiba, one of the original Sanaour Community Group that was bussed to the British School daily. She trained for a year and had to quit because her dad got sick and her family needed her. She was a promising judoka and was truly missed, so Dr. Shelley, Navneet G., and Raman found out where she lived and went there. Adiba lives in the outskirts of town where all the garbage is dumped; she lives in poverty, actually *in* the dump. Our dynamic trio talked with Adiba's family, and it was decided that the foundation would sponsor Adiba and her cousin to attend/come back to the classes. A driver has been hired to pick them up each day, take them to school, and drop them back home safe and sound, which will help change their lives just enough to make a difference. We got to work with Adiba for the demo for the DC, and she was outstanding! I am so happy to be a part of a foundation that makes this kind of change actually happen.

Our last day of teaching was very special. Navneet Jeji is the art teacher (and fabulously talented artist) at the Patiala Government College of Education, where she teaches women to be art teachers.

She worked very hard and arranged for Sonya and me to do a Gender Sensitization: Lecture, Demonstration, and Interaction self-defense class for over seventy young women at the college. It was received with valued enthusiasm. As AWMAI's (Association of Women Martial Arts Instructors) executive director, it felt like the exact way to end a trip of a lifetime: "Teaching the Teacher, Sharing Knowledge with the World"—mission statement in full.

I am home now, still processing this adventure, and working toward AWMAI's next events.

Thank you, Dr. Shelley Fernandez, for keeping Keiko Fukuda Shihan's legacy alive and for being the person who keeps fighting for justice and peace in every breath you take.

We will always have a space in our hearts that holds each and every one of those girls in Patiala.

List of Schools Sponsored by the Keiko Fukuda Judo Foundation in Patiala, India

GSSS (Government Senior Secondary School)

Old Police Line Girls' School

GJSS Multi-Purpose Junior Branch

GSSS Multi-Purpose Senior Branch

GSSS Model Towne Girls High School

GSSS Victoria Girls High School

GSSS Victoria Girls Community Youth

GSSS British Co-Ed High School

GSSS British Co-Ed Sanaour Community School for Girls

Mahiendra College (Boarding School)

GSSS Pheel Khanna Co-Ed School

GSSS Civil Lines School for Girls

GSSS Tri Pri Co-Ed School

*Patiala Government College of Education

A Letter to Keiko Fukuda Shihan (in Heaven)
by Koré Grate, November 6, 2016

When I see the signs you send,
I know you are near, supporting and guiding us …
Even though you are in a place we cannot
touch with our earthly hands or eyes.
The feeling of you and the ancestors is
unmistakable—both joyous and sad.
It is the inspiration of your dedication and kindness
That presses into our hearts, into our lives,
Carrying us further than we ever imagined.
May we express your legacy honorably and
generously to all that come on this path:
"Be strong, be gentle, be beautiful—in body, mind, and spirit."
Thank you for the life you lived.
And thank you for loving Dr. Shelley so she
could bring us on this adventure together.

TIMELINE OF KEIKO FUKUDA SHIHAN

1913	She was born in Kyobashi, Tokyo, Japan. Her grandfather is the grand jiujutsu master Hachinosuke Fukuda, who was the master of Kano Jigoro.
1935	Twenty-two years old. On the grand master Jigoro Kano's advice, she began studying judo at the women's department of the Kodokan.
1939	Twenty-six years old. She earned the first dan from the Kodokan.
1943	Thirty years old. She graduated with a degree in Japanese literature from Japan Women's University.
1946	Thirty-three years old. She earned the fourth dan from the Kodokan.
1953	Forty years old. She earned the fifth dan from the Kodokan. She visited the United States for the first time, to teach judo. She visited California and Hawaii.
1964	Fifty-one years old. She demonstrated ju-no-kata at the Tokyo Olympic Games.
1966	Fifty-three years old. She visited the United States for the second time, to teach judo.

1967	Fifty-four years old. She established Soko Joshi Judo Club with Dr. Shelley Fernandez and started teaching judo there. She taught in Canada and Australia. She came to be called "mother of world women's judo."
1972	Fifty-nine years old. She earned the sixth dan from the Kodokan.
1984	Seventy-one years old. She earned the seventh dan from the Kodokan.
1989	Seventy-six years old. She taught in France and the kingdom of Norway. The first annual International Kata Competition in America was held.
1990	Seventy-seven years old. She was awarded the Fourth Class Order of the Sacred Treasure.
1991	Seventy-eight years old. She underwent heart bypass surgery.
1992	Seventy-nine years old. She taught a judo seminar in France.
1994	Eighty-one years old. She earned the eighth dan red belt from both the Kodokan and the US Judo Federation.
2001	Eighty-eight years old. She earned the ninth dan red belt from the USA Judo Association and the USJF. She became the first and only female ninth dan holder in the world.
2004	Ninety-one years old. Her second book, *Ju-no-Kata*, was published.

2006	Ninety-three years old. She earned the ninth dan red belt as the first female judo athlete from the Kodokan. She established the Keiko Fukuda Judo Scholarship. The city of San Francisco established Keiko Fukuda Day to honor her significant contribution to the spread of judo.
2009	Ninety-six years old. She went back to Japan for the first time in thirty years. She taught at the Kodokan during her ten-day stay. Her biography, *Bow from the Heart*, was published.
2011	Ninety-eight years old. She earned the tenth dan from the USA Judo Association and the USJF. She became the first and only female tenth dan holder in the world.
2012	Ninety-nine years old. She established the Keiko Fukuda and Shelley Fernandez Girls and Women judo Foundation Inc. (www.keikofukudajudofoundation.org and keiko.judo@gmail.com). Her retrospective *Be Strong, Be Gentle, Be Beautiful,* was published in Japanese.
2013	She died on February 9, at ninety-nine years of age. Half of her ashes are at the Zen Temple Kichijoji Cemetery (3-19-17 Motokomagome Bunka-ku, Tokyo, Japan), and the other half are at Olivet Memorial Park (section B, Colma, California).
2017	Her reflections on her life, *Be Strong, Be Gentle, Be Beautiful,* is translated to English.

Keiko group lesson

GLOSSARY

bodhisattva	An enlightened being in Buddhism. Traditionally, a bodhisattva is anyone who, motivated by great compassion, has generated a spontaneous wish to attain Buddhahood for the benefit of all sentient beings.
chawan-mushi	An egg custard dish cooked with an egg mixture flavored with soy sauce, with ingredients such as shiitake mushrooms and boiled shrimp placed into a teacup-like container.
chirashi sushi	A type of sushi; assorted sashimi and colorful garnishes arranged beautifully on top of the sushi rice in a bowl.
daikon	Japanese radish.
dan	A grade of upper rank.
dojo	A training room.
Edo	The previous name of Tokyo, the capital of Japan.
Edo era	From 1603 to 1867.
gomame	Flavored dried anchovies.
judo	A modern martial art, combat and Olympic sport created in Japan in 1882 by Jigoro Kano.
jiujutsu	The martial arts for warriors.
ju-no-kata	A set of prearranged forms in judo.
Karada-sabaki	Defensive body movement.
kata	Forms of judo.

Kuzushi	Defensive body movement.
maguro sushi	A small block of rice topped with a piece of raw tuna.
marrons glacés	A confection, originating in Southern France and Northern Italy, consisting of a chestnut candied in sugar syrup and glazed.
Meiji era	From 1868 to 1912.
natto	A traditional Japanese food made from fermented soybeans.
NHK	Nippon Hōsō Kyōkai, Japan's national public broadcasting organization.
niku-jaga	A Japanese dish of meat, potatoes, and onion stewed in sweetened soy sauce.
Nodo Jiman	The title of an amateur singing contest TV program.
osen	Rice crackers. Osen is a gentle nickname of Senbei, the original name of rice crackers.
randori	Free exercise during judo practice, both defense and offense, using judo techniques.
Riai	Underlying principles behind a technique.
Ryotediri	The judo technique using the both hands.
sakaki tree	Sacred tree of Shinto.
samurai	A warrior.
satori	A Japanese Buddhist term for awakening, comprehension, understanding.
Seiza	Basic kneeling position where knees are bent 180 degrees with calves tucked under the thighs so you sit on your heels.
sensei	An instructor, a master.
shamisen	A three-stringed Japanese banjo.
shihan	A grand master, tenth degree.

Shiseido	A Japanese long-established cosmetic company.
Showa era	From 1925 to 1989.
sumo	Japanese traditional wrestling and Japan's national sport.
Taisho era	From 1912 to 1926.
(The) Great Kanto earthquake of 1923 Japan	At the time, considered the worst natural disaster ever to strike quake-prone Japan.
tofu	A food made by coagulating soy milk and then pressing the resulting curds into soft white blocks.
Tori	The judo role of throwing.
Uke	The judo role of being thrown.
Ukemi	Defensive fall.
Waza	Judo techniques.
Yawara	Techniques of gentleness in jujitsu.
Yawara-chan	The nickname for Ryoko Tamura (after her marriage, Tani), a judo athlete who holds the fourth dan. She has a record seven world titles, and she brought home the 48 kg category gold medal from the Sydney Olympics in 2000 and the Athens Olympics in 2004.
yukata	A cotton kimono for summer.

92656997R00073

Made in the USA
Middletown, DE
10 October 2018